You Should Read This Book If ...

- You are part of a couple at any stage of life with an interest in learning more about Judaism and making Judaism a greater and richer part of your life together.
- You have been practicing Judaism for many years as a family and are now empty-nesters seeking to reinvigorate your relationship and your holiday celebrations.
- You are just starting a long-term committed relationship, and you want to establish a meaningful Jewish life with your partner.
- You are in an interfaith relationship and actively trying to create a ritual life that works for you both.
- You are part of a same-sex couple and looking for a book about the Jewish holidays that affirms you and your relationship.
- You are a spiritual seeker interested in the renewal of your religious life.
- You are a Jewish community leader, rabbi, cantor, or professional, seeking new ways to introduce people to Jewish resources that speak to the issues in their lives.
- You are a therapist or pastoral care counselor who deals with couples.

Other Books
by Nancy Fuchs-Kreimer

Parenting as a Spiritual Journey:
Deepening Ordinary and Extraordinary Events into Sacred Occasions
(Jewish Lights Publishing)

Other Books
by Nancy H. Wiener

Beyond Breaking the Glass:
A Spiritual Guide to Your Jewish Wedding

Meeting at the Well:
A Jewish Spiritual Guide to Being Engaged
(co-authored with Daniel Judson)
(both URJ Press)

Judaism *for* Two

A Spiritual Guide for Strengthening and Celebrating Your Loving Relationship

Rabbi Nancy Fuchs-Kreimer
and
Rabbi Nancy H. Wiener

Foreword by Rabbi Elliot N. Dorff

For People of All Faiths, All Backgrounds

JEWISH LIGHTS Publishing

Woodstock, Vermont

Judaism for Two:
A Spiritual Guide for Strengthening and Celebrating Your Loving Relationship

2005 First Printing
© 2005 by Nancy Fuchs-Kreimer and Nancy H. Wiener

Library of Congress Cataloging-in-Publication Data
Fuchs, Nancy.
Judaism for two : a spiritual guide for strengthening and celebrating your loving relationship / Nancy Fuchs-Kreimer and Nancy H. Wiener.
p. cm.
Includes bibliographical references and index.
ISBN 1-58023-254-X (pbk.)
1. Marriage—Religious aspects—Judaism. 2. Communication in marriage. 3. Interpersonal relations—Religious aspects—Judaism. 4. Interpersonal communication. 5. Fasts and feasts—Judaism. I. Wiener, Nancy H., 1958- II. Title.
BM713.F83 2005
296.7'4—dc22
2005001851
10   9   8   7   6   5   4   3   2   1
Manufactured in the United States of America
Cover Design: Sara Dismukes
Cover Art: "Wedding Trees," a papercut by Aharon Baruch; www.abaruch.com.

Published by Jewish Lights Publishing
A Division of LongHill Partners, Inc.
Sunset Farm Offices, Route 4, P.O. Box 237
Woodstock, VT 05091
Tel: (802) 457-4000   Fax: (802) 457-4004
www.jewishlights.com

To Seth Kreimer and Judith Tax,
our partners, for whom and to whom we are grateful.

Contents

Foreword

In the last century, we have witnessed significant changes in our society in matters of gender and sex. We have gone from the inability of women to vote to many women serving in Congress, two on the United States Supreme Court and one running as a major party candidate for vice president. We have gone from little formal education for girls—or for boys, for that matter—to a very high percentage of North American Jews engaged in extended education into their late twenties. We have gone from women staying at home to raise children and helping their husbands in running the business when they could to women having their own careers. And we have gone from Victorian sexual morals to no laws at all governing consenting adults in their private, sexual behavior.

These changes have also engendered major changes in our family patterns. A hundred years ago people lived in extended families, with parents, aunts, uncles, and cousins nearby. Now we live in nuclear families, with relatives often far away. Moreover, the American population generally and the Jewish population in particular now includes many single adults, divorced people, single parents, gay and lesbian couples, intermarried couples, blended families, and unmarried couples living together. This book addresses all relationships—traditional and non-traditional.

It also adopts a new methodology. How do you make the Jewish tradition relevant to Jews who live in vastly different circumstances from those prevalent among Jews until just one hundred years ago? This problem affects many aspects of our Jewish lives—medical ethics is a very clear example of this problem—but perhaps the most important area to consider is our own personal lives. Some (myself included) have written books attempting to apply the Jewish tradition to the moral issues that modernity has created for our personal lives. Others have written how-to books about Judaism, explaining how to carry out the traditional rituals. Some such books, like those by Ron Wolfson, my colleague at the University of Judaism, have specifically suggested ways for modern families to make the traditional rituals more meaningful for everyone involved. This book, though, does a unique thing: it uses Jewish holy days to address the many tensions and challenges of modern life for Jews in any of the new relationships—empty-nesters without extended families nearby, heterosexuals in long-term relationships but not married, interfaith couples, same-sex couples, and simply those unfamiliar with Jewish holiday rituals and the personal meanings they can have. In doing this, Rabbis Nancy Fuchs-Kreimer and Nancy H. Wiener have done us a real service, for they have shown us all how the holidays can be an effective therapy for the personal challenges of the modern world while retaining their traditional, communal meanings.

Thus readers should be aware, as the authors tell us in the Introduction, that theirs is not only a lesson for a new audience, but a new type of learning altogether. They cite the early twentieth-century Jewish theologian Franz Rosenzweig, who declared then that "A new learning is about to be born.... It is a learning in reverse order. A learning that no longer starts from the Torah and leads to life, but the other way around: from life back to the Torah." *Judaism for Two* is indeed that type of learning and, as such, is well attuned to modern Jews.

Our ancestors from the Middle Ages and the early modern period grew up in almost exclusively Jewish (and sometimes physically enclosed) communities, and they presumed that God required each Jew to abide by the Torah and the Jewish tradition. As a result, the Torah was their starting point, and they saw their life's task as living in response to it.

The Enlightenment, however, changed all of that. Nations shaped by Enlightenment ideas were based on individual rights. Although the practice took time to catch up with the theory, Jews living in such societies could live anywhere they wanted. Furthermore, they interacted with citizens of other religious and ethnic backgrounds not only in business, but in education, government, science, economics, and culture—and they did so as equals. Philosophically, the starting point for modern Jews was no longer the Torah, but their own individual rights. As a result, if Jews were to identify with the Jewish tradition and make it part of their lives, they had to be persuaded that they should give up their rights to eat certain foods and to use certain days of the week and year as they wish in favor of observing Jewish rituals and holidays. They had to find personal meaning in them. God's command could no longer compete with individuals' rights to choose any form of religious beliefs and practices they wanted, including none at all. Contemporary Jews are often much more open to delving into their tradition than their parents were, and they are even willing to speak in terms of God and spirituality. But the vast majority of modern Jews will not see Jewish traditions as authoritative for them simply because the Torah says that God commands them to follow these rules. They must instead be convinced that Jewish practices can enrich their own lives. This book is a stellar example of how Jewish holy days can fit that modern agenda.

Elliot N. Dorff
University of Judaism;
author of *Love Your Neighbor and Yourself: A Jewish Approach to Modern Personal Ethics*

Preface

We have written this book for you. You may be an empty-nester, searching for ways to renew your connection to Judaism, or you may be a young couple just embarking on this adventure and interested in establishing patterns that will support you along the way. Perhaps you are with a new partner after years with another. You may be a Jew who is eager to learn more about your heritage, convinced that it will yield riches for you. Or you may be more ambivalent or even skeptical, but will be happy, though a bit surprised, if it turns out that Jewish tradition is relevant to something as important to you as your marriage. You may be in an interfaith relationship, where Judaism is one of two or more traditions you draw on for inspiration. You may simply be a spiritual seeker, curious to learn new perspectives.

We also have written this book for ourselves. Nancy K. and Seth have been together since 1972. When they were fumbling their way through their lives as young parents, they found in the traditions of Judaism a rich mine of gestures and words, of rituals and acts, of times and seasons. The values and the practices became the scaffolding of their lives. Just as the Jewish holiday cycle shaped their year, the Sabbath gave form to their week. They bound themselves to these "rules for the road," wanting to create a coherent heritage to pass on to their children. Blessing their children at the Sabbath table each Friday night became a weekly reminder of holiness, a sturdy vessel to carry their aspirations and their love. Nancy wrote her book *Parenting as a Spiritual Journey:*

Deepening Ordinary and Extraordinary Events into Sacred Occasions, reporting on the wisdom she learned from parents she met along the way.

When their children began to leave home, Seth and Nancy started planning for the next stage. They searched the "Relationships" shelves of several downtown bookstores, returning home with piles of books. They learned about fighting fair and listening skills and scheduling couples' meetings. But they wondered if picking apart their relationship in the earnest ways recommended would really leave them with a stronger and more joyous bond. Even books that prescribed "having fun with your partner" or planning a "date night" made it all sound like dreaded homework!

Nancy W. and Judith have been together since 1986. When they began to plan for their *Kiddush Ahavah,* the ceremony celebrating the sanctity of their love, there were no books that spoke directly to their lives as Jewish lesbians, that offered guidance in the barely charted territory of same-sex religious ceremonies. Their myriad questions and concerns were answered through trial and error and guesswork. This led Nancy to write two books, *Beyond Breaking the Glass: A Spiritual Guide to Your Jewish Wedding* and *Meeting at the Well: A Jewish Spiritual Guide to Being Engaged* (with co-author Daniel Judson), about liberal Jewish marriage and the spiritual and personal preparation involved. They are written for both same-sex and straight couples.

Today Judith and Nancy are entering a new phase in their life together. They wonder how Judaism's family focus will speak to them as two middle-aged Jews in a long-term committed relationship without children. They expect to continue blessing each other each Friday night, taking their reflective walks as the High Holy Days approach, and working in a soup kitchen on Christmas Day, and they are eager to discover how Jewish holiday myths and metaphors can continue to add meaning to their life as a couple.

We know that there are many religious books that deal with relationships. Some of them offer a generic spirituality that provides insights without the specificity of any particular religious context, metaphors, or practices. Their intentions, however beautiful in the abstract, are difficult to remember in the moment: "Be kind!" But when? "Appreciate your partner!" But how? Others are written from the perspective of traditional practitioners of a specific religious tradition (usually Jewish or Christian) and assume roles and rules that may not sound much like the lives many of us are actually living.

In this book you will find Jewish holidays presented in a new way, highlighting practices and concepts that speak to you as a couple. The Jewish cycle of Sabbaths and holidays can offer a valuable gift to you and your partner, year in and year out: the gift of sacred time, time together to focus on the blessings of your relationship. We invite you to study some of the texts, engage in some of the suggested activities. Most important, we hope you will use this book as a springboard to think about your relationship. As the seasons of the year pass, may you find renewed meaning in your time together.

Options for Reading This Book

- Read it cover to cover by yourself as a catalyst for your own thinking and further study.
- Read it with your partner as a way to stimulate discussion. The exercises are ideas to get you started. You and your partner are the best ones to decide what will work for you.
- Use it as a resource as each holiday approaches.
- Create a study group with other couples (and a teacher, if you like) in order to engage with the material together and to support one another in your growth.

Acknowledgments

We are particularly grateful to Judith Tax, who devoted endless hours to editing, suggesting rewrites, copyediting, and formatting the entire manuscript for publication.

We are grateful to the women who participated in our initial focus groups: Claire Levi, Marsha Weinraub, Helen Feinberg, Janis Smith, Doris Ferleger, Robin Heller, Dian Ajl, Adina Newberg, Cindy Perkiss, Reverend Flo Gelo, and Sue Hoffman.

We also appreciate those who read parts of the manuscript: Rena Kreimer, Seth Kreimer, Carol Towarnicky, Carl Norden, Rabbi Marsha Pik-Nathan, Rabbi Marjorie Berman, Judy Petsonk, Patricia Bradshaw, and Liz Abrams-Morley; and those who read and commented on the entire manuscript: Gari Weilbacher, Joyce Norden, Andee Hochman, Rabbi Sue Levi Elwell, Kathy Hirsh-Pasek, Betsy Teutsch, Ruth Friedkin, Betsy Stone, Leslie and Eric Cohen-Rubury, and Rachel Bush.

Rabbi Melissa Klein and Sarah Rubin helped find and check references.

Our gratitude to the Nathan Cummings Foundation for its support of SeRaF (Senior Resource Faculty), a joint project of the National Center for Jewish Healing and the Kalsman Institute of Judaism and Health (HUC–JIR), under whose auspices this book was first conceived.

Our editors at Jewish Lights Publishing, Emily Wichland and Sally Freedman, offered an unusual degree of dedication to the editorial process.

Stuart M. Matlins, publisher of Jewish Lights, is a man with a vision for the renewal of Jewish life; we are honored to be part of his work.

Introduction

The world is created anew in goodness each morning.

—From the traditional morning prayer service

When their children were young, Linda and Eric thought they were as busy as they could possibly be. Now, with just the two of them at home, they rush from the office to the gym to newfound quests. Linda has recently begun to meditate, and Eric has become passionate about politics. Their conversations often consist of little more than information transfers. They know that their commitment to a life together is a holy enterprise that they need to cherish, nurture, and protect, and they want to celebrate their life in ways that deepen their connection. But with no particular date on the calendar, this usually falls to the bottom of the "to do" list. When they are together (and not too exhausted), they agree that while they may not have time to consciously create their bond "anew each morning," they do need to carve out appointed times for renewal.

But time is only part of their problem. Eric and Linda live in an age that is challenging for long-term love. Roles are in flux, and the communities that once would have supported their lives together are now fragmented. At the same time, the expectations the culture places on marriage are immense. Eric and Linda are unlikely to succeed at being each other's best friend, soul mate, *and* lover every day. Nevertheless, they plan to remain faithful to their relationship. They want to know how to live gracefully through the years with another human being and grow together in spirit. On Valentine's Day Eric buys Linda flowers, and on their anniversary they go out to dinner, but those traditions are not enough. Appointed times of connection need to be more than just "date nights" or vacations; they need to occur within a larger context of meaning.

Jewish holidays can serve as fixed times for couples to strengthen their loving relationships. More than just calendar commitments, the holidays carry with them a view of what is important in life, a set of assumptions that challenge and deepen the way we think about relationships. According to Jewish tradition, the world stands on three things: ritual, learning, and acts of loving-kindness (*Mishnah Avot* 1:2). These three "pillars" of Jewish life have surprising insights to offer when applied to our lives as couples. In this book you will find new ways to think about your loving partnership in light of the Jewish holidays. At the end of each chapter you will also find suggestions for ways to include ritual, learning, and loving-kindness in your lives together.

The Holiday Cycle

You have given us appointed times for joy ... and for remembering.

—From the festival blessing

Rabbi Abraham Joshua Heschel described Shabbat, and by extension the holidays, as "palaces in time." More recently, Rabbi Michael Strassfeld referred to these special days as "inns," lodgings for us as we "travel" through the year. These inns, he taught, are not for resting but for waking up to our lives.

Most of us have never thought about the holidays as a

means of awakening to our lives as a couple. Our celebrations often focus on Jewish history, connection to family and community, or passing the heritage to the next generation. But the Jewish holidays can also become "inns" or "palaces" in which couples can spend time together. Each holiday presents us with an opportunity to focus on what is significant in our lives, to enhance what is sacred in our connection with our partners. They provide a structure on which to hang our best intentions. Our relationships often "get away from us" for lack of attention. The holidays give us a framework that can call us back from drifting.

For many of us the holidays are already saturated with meaning. Our recollections may be of childhood delight or of family quarrels. While all that history may seem like a distraction, it also reminds us of an important truth. As couples, we each have our share of victories and losses. How do we hold them in our memories as we move forward with hope to what can be? Each Jewish holiday carries its own unique perspective on that question. As we look through the lenses the holidays provide, we see different ways we can construct a new narrative out of our own stories.

For traditional Jews, Shabbat (*Shabbes* in Yiddish) does not simply arrive. Rather, they talk about "*making* Shabbes." Since the seventh day of the week comes around no matter what, that may seem an odd way of speaking. But we do have to *make* Shabbat, just as we have to *make* each of our holidays, through conscious choices and actions.

The same is true of love. When people talk about "*making* love," they usually mean sex. But we can *make* love, just as we can *make* Shabbat—through our choices. And making the holidays can help us make love. The three traditional pillars of ritual, study, and loving-kindness can support your relationship as well as the world.

Celebrations/*Minhagim*

I don't know exactly what a prayer is.
I do know how to pay attention.

—Mary Oliver

If you and your partner get into bed every night, watch the news, and turn off the light, that is a routine. If you consciously choose to spend the last minutes of your day together in that way, mindful of the rhythm and tone of your sharing, that is a ritual. Ritual elevates a routine by turning it into a celebration. The Hebrew word for ritual is *minhag*, which comes from the verb "to lead" and has come to mean "the way it is done." But ritual is more than just the way something is done; it is choosing to notice what we do and making it special. Birthday parties and senior proms are *minhagim* in our culture. Another way to translate *minhagim* is "celebrations."

Most likely you began your life as a couple with a ritual of some kind. You took that moment of transition and held it up to the light so that it reflected something larger, whether it was community, tradition, or the Source of Life. That instinct can be carried into your daily, weekly, and yearly routines.

Jewish rituals can be understood as spiritual practices, which may or may not conform to the Jewish law from which they often grow. Each week Susan and Jo look forward to Friday night. Jo's shift at the hospital ends at eight, and she doesn't get home until after nine. Rather than light the Shabbat candles eighteen minutes before sunset, as tradition prescribes, Susan waits until Jo gets home. Lighting the candles together is important to them. It is the moment in their week when—by appointment!—they acknowledge the blessing of their life together.

Every holiday offers new opportunities for rituals. Some are ancient, others relatively recent; some are waiting to be invented by you. *The rituals in this book are not recipes but examples.* The approach outlined here encourages you to take the most creative look possible at rituals. The tradition is a rich resource, not a straightjacket. In describing the Passover seder, poet Linda Pastan wrote, "I set my table with metaphor." When Alan and Jane created a "seder plate" for their anniversary, placing on it items with special symbolic meaning to their marriage (sea shells from Cape Cod, protest buttons from the sixties, and photos of their children), they set the table with their own metaphors. How can celebrations from the past become vehicles for you to enhance the days and months of your life together? How can you create new opportunities on a daily and weekly basis, as well as for annual events?

Rituals are symbolic acts that often begin with a blessing. A blessing is a pause to reflect, to note the privilege of being alive and present in that moment, whether or not we call what we are doing prayer. The Talmud records this blessing by Rabbi Ben Zoma:

> What effort Adam had to make before he could obtain bread to eat! He plowed, he sowed, he reaped, he bound, he threshed, he winnowed … he kneaded and baked…. Whereas I rise in the morning and find all these things done for me!
>
> —*Berakhot 58a*

Saying an original blessing out loud may make you self-conscious. You might find it easier to start with prescribed words. Before eating, for example, it is traditional to say: *Barukh atah Adonai, Eloheinu Melekh haolam, hamotzi lehem min haaretz*; We praise you, God, Source of Life, who brings forth bread from the earth. Before lighting candles on Shabbat, the traditional blessing is: *Barukh atah Adonai, Eloheinu Melekh haolam, asher kidshanu b'mitzvotav v'tzivanu l'hadlik ner shel Shabbat;* We praise you, God, Source of Life, who makes us holy with your mitzvot and commands us to kindle the Shabbat lights. Because the ancient formulas carry with them the faith and hope of the generations who used them, you can think of them as the "conservation of spiritual energy."

Traditional Jewish blessings are addressed to God, the "Sovereign" of the world. That language reminds us that ritual is also a connection to that which is beyond us, to the Mystery in which we live. Over time you may add words of your own to the tradition, or perhaps you prefer to begin with your own language. You may simply want to take a moment of silence together and center yourselves before you begin your ritual. The essential thing is to slow down and, like Ben Zoma, acknowledge with gratitude the gifts in your lives.

Learning with a Partner/<u>H</u>evruta

May your study be passionate,
And meanings bear more meanings
*   Until life itself arrays itself to you*
As a dazzling wedding feast.

—Danny Siegel (based on *Berakhot* 17a)

Do you like to be right? Most people do. We typically see our different perspectives as obstacles to be overcome, whether we are arguing about whom to vote for in the next election or the best place to store ripe bananas. Often our first instinct may be to insist that we are correct and our partner wrong. There is, however, another way to view our differences.

Think of the last time you went to a movie with your partner. You sat through the same film, but when you walked out you each commented on different details, focused on different characters, scenes, dialogue. Each of you had heard, understood, and interpreted the experience in a different way. Through your discussion you became aware of aspects of the film that you had not noticed, and each of you was exposed to new understandings. By the end of your conversation you had seen a different movie from the one you would have seen had you gone alone.

For centuries Jews have studied sacred texts with partners. This practice, known as *hevruta,* is a classic mode of Jewish scholarly life. Two people sit together and read a text aloud, discuss it, analyze it, relate it to other texts, and share relevant illustrations from their own lives or stories they have heard. When they disagree, they set out their reasons, side by side. The Talmud is sixty-three books' worth of *hevruta* sessions, conducted over many centuries. Why would a record of arguments become a sacred text, second only to the Bible in importance? Perhaps to show us that truth has multiple faces and is best discovered in conversation with others.

At the end of each chapter in this book you will find very short texts, both from Jewish tradition and other sources, which you and your partner can use as study material. In addition, you can read the entire book together in a *hevruta* mode. As you listen to one another in a spirit of openness and trust, you can learn more about each other and yourselves, articulate values, and enjoy the pleasure of exchanging ideas. Through study, analysis, imagination, and sharing of inherited traditions (personal, literary, cultural, and religious), you can engage with one another through engaging the text.

You may want to think about how you and your partner frame your study time together. Perhaps you will choose a particular place in your house that will serve as your *hevruta* corner. Will you use chairs that you find especially comfortable? Many couples find they enjoy studying together sitting up in bed.

There is a traditional Jewish blessing for study: *Barukh atah Adonai, Eloheinu Melekh haolam, asher kidshanu b'mitzvotav v'tzivanu laasok b'divrei Torah;* We praise you, God, Source of Life, who makes us holy with your mitzvot and commands us to engage with the words of Torah. While it may seem strange to say those words before studying a secular poem, think of Torah as "teaching" in the broadest possible sense. If the traditional prayer doesn't work for you, you can use your own words. Karen and Jeff start their *hevruta* sessions with a brief prayer in which they express the hope that they will listen to one another with generosity and that their learning will be a blessing for them and for the world.

Study in *hevruta* should deepen your bond and remind you to revel in your differences. Applying this perspective to our lives is the real challenge. Every day our long-term committed relationships offer us an opportunity to practice the skills of *hevruta*. The "texts" are everywhere: the morning paper, an interaction with a repairman, the problems of a child or an aging parent. The concept of *hevruta* reminds us that there is more than one right way to see things; something is lost if we and our partners always see things the same way. The Talmud tells how a voice from heaven resolved a dispute between rabbis by saying, "These and these are the words of the living God" (*Eruvin* 13b). Or, as a refrigerator magnet puts it, "You can either be right or be in relationship."

Reaching Out/*Gemilut Hesed*

We are here to do
And through doing to learn
and through learning to know
and through knowing to experience wonder …
and through attention
to see what needs to be done.

—Rami Shapiro (based on *Pirkei Avot* 5:27)

Jewish tradition sees ritual and text study as points of departure. No Jewish celebration is complete without some act leading outward to the world. Connection with the Divine comes through deeds. To "walk after God," says the Talmud, means to do what God does. In the Torah, God clothes the naked (Adam and Eve) and buries the dead (Moses), and by extension, so should we (*Sotah* 29a). As Rabbi Israel Salanter expressed it, "The physical life of another is an obligation of my spiritual life."

Deeds of caring are known in Hebrew as *gemilut ḥesed*, literally "the doling out of loving-kindness." Traditional examples include providing a dowry for a poor bride, visiting the sick, offering hospitality. Such acts can become central to the spirituality of your relationship in two ways: They can be at the heart of how you treat one another; and they can focus your gaze outward to the world and its needs.

Acts of loving-kindness begin not with one's own rights but with another's needs. The quintessential act of loving-kindness is to accompany someone's body to the grave, for that person cannot possibly repay you. Whether our kindness is extended to the person in our house for whom we fetch the newspaper on a cold morning (again!) or an orphan on the other side of the world, this is an essential Jewish practice.

When we engage in acts of loving-kindness in our homes and in the world they mutually reinforce one another. For some of us, giving to the one we love is easy, but we need to learn how to stretch ourselves toward the world as well. For some of us it is easier to act generously toward a stranger in the street than toward the person within our home. Yet the same acts of loving-kindness that you cultivate toward those in the greater community are also the ones you will want to cultivate toward each other. Acts of loving-kindness are among the most powerful activities for couples to share. In working to realize your common values in the world around you—mindful of the way they figure into your life as a couple—you can enlarge the meaning of your time together.

For celebrations and learning together, tradition prescribes the ritual pause of a blessing. For acts of loving-kindness, however, there is no traditional blessing. Commentators have suggested several reasons for this. First, thanking God for the opportunity to help a person in need may make it seem that we are thankful for the person's neediness. Second, by making a religious experience out of our act of compassion, we may objectify the activity or focus on our own virtue instead of on the person in need. Finally, nothing—not even the minute or two it would take to say a blessing—should delay us in performing these acts.

Can I Use This Book on My Own?

It is possible that you and your partner are reading this book as a shared project, or that you have found a group of couples who are studying it together, perhaps with a teacher. Most likely, however, you are reading this by yourself, and that's fine, too. Trying to make your partner participate in activities that he or she resists is not a good recipe for building intimacy. You can begin thinking about and using many of the ideas in this book on your own. Relationships are systems, and any change—however small—by one person will eventually affect the whole. If you make a change in ritual practice, in study, or in engaging with the world, your relationship with your partner will change as well.

For example, suppose you like the idea of "giving it a rest," inspired by Shabbat. You decide that next time you and your partner are together for a few hours you will avoid all the following "work": analyzing, philosophizing, requesting more information, finding solutions. You resolve that no matter what

your partner says, you will respond in a "Shabbat-like" manner.
Suppose you go out to dinner, and
your partner says, "I'm exhausted.
I had a hard day at work." Rather
than offering suggestions for solv-
ing the problem, you might respond sympathetically, "You do
work hard." After an evening of
such treatment, your partner will
be having a bit of a "Shabbat" despite not having signed up for it,
and is unlikely to complain.

Perhaps the concept of _hevruta_
appeals to you, but your partner
scoffs at the idea of sitting down
and reading a text with a set of
questions attached. Nevertheless,
the next time you are at the break-

But there is always an-
other opinion! In light
of the importance of so-
cial action in the lives of
many contemporary Jews,
the Reform movement
has created a new bless-
ing: *Barukh atah Adonai,
Eloheinu Melekh haolam,
asher kidshanu
b'mitzvotav v'tzivanu
l'takein haolam.* We
praise you, God, Source
of Life, who makes us
holy with your mitzvot
and commands us to re-
pair the world.

fast table and you begin to discuss a newspaper article, you can
treat it as a _hevruta_ opportunity. If your partner has a different view
from your own, you can make a conscious decision to respond in
the _hevruta_ spirit of give-and-take, reveling in differences rather
than trying to establish who is right and who is wrong.

You can also seek out a _hevruta_ partner who is not your life
partner. If you and a friend are both interested in enhancing your
relationships with your spouses, you might decide to meet every
couple of weeks over coffee to study together. You can read texts
at the same time as you talk about the challenges of your relationships. You can support one another in your learning and
growth.

And finding new ways to reach out beyond yourselves can
enrich your shared life as a couple. Your partner may be more

eager to celebrate Pesah by giving away food than by studying the Haggadah. On the other hand, he may find the idea of giving blood together on your children's birthday just plain strange. No matter. The specific practices are less important than the questions you ask yourself: How can our commitments to the world become a source of connection for us as a couple? How can our engagement outside our home deepen our understanding of how we act toward one another?

In the musical *Fiddler on the Roof,* Tevye surprises Goldie with the question, "Do you love me?" It takes a while, but Goldie finally concludes that she does. For twenty-five years she has fought with him, starved with him, shared his bed. As she puts it, "If that's not love, what is?" For these traditional Jews, observing the holidays was simply "what God expected them to do." Torah was a given; love was an afterthought.

In American culture today, the question of love is front and center. Most books written for couples focus on you: how happy you are, how satisfying your relationship can be. In this book we begin with you and your relationship, but we do not end there. As Franz Rosenzweig said:

> A new learning is about to be born.... It is a learning in reverse order. A learning that no longer starts from the Torah and leads into life, but the other way around: from life, back to the Torah.

As you embark on this journey "from life," you should not feel limited by the calendar. You may decide to rededicate your home in the middle of the summer rather than at Hanukkah. You may draw upon insights from Yom Kippur whenever forgiveness is an issue. What Samuel Dresner wrote about the Sabbath applies to all the holidays: "The Sabbath is not a theory to be contemplated, a concept to be debated, or an idea to be toyed with. It is a day, a day filled with hours and minutes and seconds."

As you consider each of the holidays, you will have an opportunity to connect with it in some new ways. The concepts and messages are waiting for you to explore. And the hours and minutes and seconds are waiting to be blessed.

Hanukkah

In December, on the darkest nights of the year, Jews celebrate the eight-day festival of Hanukkah. Hanukkah, which literally means "dedication," refers to the rededication of the Temple in Jerusalem after the successful uprising of a small band of Jewish rebels against foreign rulers in 168 BCE. The story is told in the Book of Maccabees, which describes the rebellion led by Judah Maccabee. A different explanation for the holiday, written down several centuries later in the Talmud, focuses on the story of a single cruse of oil that lasted for the full eight days of the Temple dedication ceremony.

Today the central ritual of Hanukkah takes place at home. On each of the eight nights of the holiday, family members light a nine-branched candelabrum (menorah or *hanukkiyah*), which is usually placed in a window.

There are three blessings that accompany this ritual. The first thanks God for the commandment to light the lights of Hanukkah: *Barukh atah Adonai, Eloheinu Melekh haolam, asher kidshanu b'mitzvotav v'tzivanu l'hadlik ner shel Hanukkah.* The second thanks God for the miracles experienced by our ancestors: *Barukh atah Adonai, Eloheinu Melekh haolam, she-asah nisim laavoteinu bayamim haheim bazman hazeh.* And the third, the *Sheheheyanu*, which is said on the first night only, thanks God "for giving us life, for sustaining us, and for bringing us to this day": *Barukh atah Adonai, Eloheinu Melekh haolam, Sheheheyanu v'kiy'manu v'higiyanu lazman hazeh.*

CHAPTER ONE

Telling Our Story, Dedicating Our Space: <u>H</u>anukkah

I have walked through many lives,
some of them my own,
and I am not who I was,
though some principle of being
abides, from which I struggle
not to stray …
Though I lack the art to decipher it,
no doubt the next chapter
in my book of transformations
is already written.
I am not done with my changes.

—**Stanley Kunitz**

Every relationship begins with hope. Two people take the risk of becoming involved, becoming vulnerable. When they make a long-term commitment to one another, they are taking a leap of faith: faith that they can grow and change together, faith in a future they cannot foresee. Like lighting a lamp in the darkest moments of winter, kindling the flame of commitment and rekindling it each year are signs of the miracles, wonders, and power of faith that can sustain you in an unpredictable and often very dark world. In a long-term relationship, nothing makes any sense without hope. And each forward step rekindles faith in the possibility of something new. The Jewish festival of lights, which began as a rededication of the sanctuary in Jerusalem, carries messages for us as couples: messages about the telling of our stories, about hope and identity, and about how we dedicate our own homes as sanctuaries even as we remind ourselves to reach out beyond them with our gifts.

Telling Our Stories and Finding New Meanings

We all tell stories about our lives—our lives as individuals, our lives as families, our lives as a people. The events we include in the narrative and the meanings we give to them change over time, as we change, as our audience changes, as our understanding of ourselves and the world changes. Each time something significant occurs, we either work it comfortably into the narrative-as-we've-told-it, fitting it into our existing sense of meaning, or find a way to tell the entire narrative in a new way to accommodate the new information. Either way, the process involves reinterpreting old information, drawing on new information, and creating a new focus and locus for the larger story.

Hanukkah's story has been told in different ways by Jews of different eras. The earliest version celebrated the rededication of the Temple after a military victory. The talmudic Rabbis focused on a story about a single cruse of oil that miraculously burned for eight days.

Modern Zionists emphasized the issue of national liberation in a secular song that asserts, "Now all of Israel must join together and redeem itself."

The significant recasting of Hanukkah can be a guide to us, inspiring us to think more openly about our own stories. It reminds us that we can change the story we tell ourselves about our past. For couples, Hanukkah can be a time to consider the story we tell about our relationship, how it has changed, and how we might tell it differently. Ascribing new meanings to past events helps us live more comfortably with our past and our present, and enables us to look toward the future with hope. Hanukkah's changing narratives encourage us to reconsider our own old stories in light of our new insights.

What is Hanukkah? Our Rabbis taught: On the twenty-fifth day of Kislev the days of Hanukkah begin.... For when the Greeks entered the Temple they defiled all the oil. When the Hasmoneans defeated them, they found one cruse of oil which had the seal of the high priest but it had only enough for one day's lighting. Yet a miracle happened and they lit the lamp for eight days. The following year those days were set aside as a festival with songs of praise and thanksgiving (*Shabbat* 21b).

From soon after you met, you began to tell your story as a couple. At first it focused on how and when you met and the early stages of your relationship. As time passed, you had more moments to retell, and the significance of some of those early "key" moments changed. Think back to how you talked about your relationship to new acquaintances shortly after you met. Compare that to the way you talk about those early days now: the adjectives you use about each other; the way you describe the trajectory of your relationship; the meaning you give to your meeting and deciding to make a life together. With each retelling, with the change of even one detail, you are redefining or re-creating your relationship. With each change there is loss, but also the potential for gaining new meaning. Each change is an implicit commitment to going on; each becomes a new narrative and sometimes a new celebration.

Despite the radical differences among the Hanukkah stories, many Jews have come to understand this holiday and its rituals best by fusing some or all of them together. They become a single, layered story, with some details diminishing in importance and others being emphasized and embellished, depending on the desires and the circumstances of the teller. It is the same for us and our personal stories. As our understanding of ourselves and our relationships develops, our stories emphasize different details and meanings, often becoming a single layered story with its own focus or message.

Who can retell the things that befell us? Who can count them? In ev'ry age, a hero or sage came to our aid. Hark! In days of yore in Israel's ancient land, Maccabeus led the faithful band. Now all Israel must as one arise, Redeem itself through deeds and sacrifice.

—Mi Yimaleil

Even the way we tell ourselves about Hanukkah can change over time. When their first child was born, Jean and Mike agreed to make their family's celebration of Hanukkah one of the highlights of the year. For Jean it was a way to transform their home, its sights and smells, into a festive space. For Mike, who had been raised Methodist, it was a way to re-create, albeit with a different focus, the joy of the season he had known while growing up. Now, their children grown, Jean and Mike are facing their first Hanukkah on their own. They have no satisfactory way to explain, even to themselves, how and why they will celebrate. It's easy enough to take the old menorah from the cabinet and light the candles, but they really want to figure out what meaning it has for them, as individuals and as a couple, at this stage of their life.

On a holiday such as Hanukkah, which has pervasive associations with children, finding meaningful ways to celebrate as adults with or without children can be a challenge. But among Judaism's more interesting teachings is one that says that finding a novel interpretation or teaching within the tradition is a sign of an agile mind and a committed heart. Whatever Mike and Jean end up doing, their new practice will become part of their ongoing life story.

The story of hope connected to H̲anukkah can become part of our own stories, sustaining our spirits. The rabbinic version of H̲anukkah focuses on a miracle. But when did the miracle occur? Was it the eighth night when "miracle oil" was still burning, contrary to expectation? Or was it the first night, when the weary Jews, seeing the devastation of the Temple, lacking any assurances concerning the future, lit the lamp anyway, hoping it would suffice?

For Marty and Emily, this story and its message of hope held a special meaning. Marty was subject to bouts of depression. All would be going well and then, with no apparent catalyst, his spirits would plummet. The first time this happened Emily was scared, and she too felt hopeless, helpless. With professional help, they both learned how to manage his depressions. During the dark periods, Marty felt Emily's constancy as a powerful and positive influence. Emily and Marty recognized that while he wasn't interested in seeing other people, she would need to continue with her social life, and that was OK. Each H̲anukkah Marty and Emily stand quietly in the darkness together before lighting the first candle, contemplating what it means to trust in the dark, to begin the light-making, even without guarantees. After their time in darkness, one or the other purposefully lights the candles, reminding them of their recurring experiences of hope finally breaking through.

Identity and Assimilation

For some of us, it will be H̲anukkah's story of identity and assimilation that resonates most personally and profoundly. In contemporary America, particularly at the winter holiday season, some Jews feel the need to protect their distinct identity, isolating themselves from the non-Jewish world as much as possible. For others, H̲anukkah's position in the calendar has created popular pressure to turn it into a "Jewish Christmas," raising issues of identity and assimilation. Still others want nothing more than to disappear into the throng, to participate in all the festivities. Somewhere in the middle are the rest of us—muddling through, trying to find our own comfort zone where we can share in the broader culture and still maintain our own identities.

Similar tensions exist within our relationships. As couples, we work hard to create a shared world, even while maintaining our individual sense of self. Within the context of our relationships, we want to strengthen the connections we have in common while honoring our individuality. We want to retain the things that make a "me," even as we create a "we."

Some issues are easy: Your family always served brisket on Hanukkah, his served mushroom soup; in your shared home you serve both. Others are more challenging, because the issues are more fundamental and compromise is not easy to come by: Your husband is committed to living in a city, but you feel more at home in a suburban setting. Between any two extremes lies most of life. And how we eventually tell the stories of our choices helps us to re-create our relationship and articulate its evolving meaning.

These tensions are especially prominent in a home with two religious traditions. When a Jew and a Christian commit to a shared life, the time surrounding Hanukkah and Christmas may be the most challenging time of the year. Jerry and Adina thought they had it all worked out at their wedding. Although Jerry was not planning to convert to Judaism, they had agreed to "have a Jewish home." The first year of their marriage Jerry casually referred to their spending Christmas with his family. Adina was shocked. "I'm Jewish. I love your family, but I can't be in a house with a Christmas tree, and I can't participate with your family in celebrating a Christian holiday." Jerry was equally taken aback. He thought their commitment was about their shared home. He was happy to adjust to celebrating Hanukkah, to the lack of a Christmas tree in their home, but he had assumed that Adina would be able to adjust when they visited his family.

No therapist or clergyperson could give Adina and Jerry an arbitrary "correct" solution to their dilemma. They had to forge a compromise that reflected and honored each one's integrity. And, as they learned over the years, their compromise was never ironclad; it shifted as the circumstances of their lives changed.

Even couples from similar religious backgrounds are raised within family cultures that nurture specific ways of defining themselves in the world. Their ways of expressing religious tradition and celebrating holidays differ according to their family histories. Their ways of defining and expressing love and commitment may differ as well. Within the context of your relationship, it is important to strengthen the connections you have in common, while not relinquishing your own identities.

Paula and Ray were, as their friends put it, "fused at the hip" during their first years of marriage. They went everywhere together. They couldn't imagine spending a vacation apart. This worked well as long as Ray chose not to tell her that he preferred doing something else. He thought this was the best way to keep the relationship strong. When he realized, however, that he was no longer spending time with close friends and he had let mountaineering drop out of his life, he saw he wasn't being true to himself. He was losing touch with significant parts of his identity. It was a long, slow, and sometimes painful process for them to talk this through together, but now, years later, Paula helps him pack for his annual mountain trek. Today Paula and Ray know that time spent alone, expressing their unique talents and interests, is as much an expression of their love for each other as their times together.

David and Joy shared all sorts of passions and interests. They could always agree on vacation destinations. However, when it came to planning the details, they were of opposite temperaments. David loved to spend months planning every moment of a trip. For

Joy the fun of travel was in not knowing where they would be the next day. Their first few vacations as a married couple were horrible. They lurched back and forth between their two approaches, both of them highly critical of the time they spent doing it the other's way, both feeling threatened that their own path was being challenged or might be obliterated entirely. As they became more secure with each other and within themselves, they realized that compromises did not have to threaten their identities. They found that they could enjoy the other's style of vacationing. Joy could appreciate David's thoughtful planning, and David could exult in Joy's spontaneity, as long as they both respected their differences.

This process varies for every couple. There is a story of a dispute between two famous Rabbis, Hillel and Shammai, about the way the Hanukkah candles should be lit. Hillel said that we should light one candle on the first night and then add a candle each night that follows. Shammai believed that we should work our way down from lighting all the candles to lighting just one (*Shabbat* 21a). While Hillel's preference became normative, it was never identified as the only or "right" way to light the candles. Either way might be acceptable, depending on the community, the era, and the location. Integrity means not picking the "right" balance in some objective sense, but negotiating together the balance that feels right for you. Even the ways we reconcile our differences become part of our larger story, helping us appreciate how we and our relationships change over time.

Dedicating and Sanctifying Our Spaces

Everyplace is good; home is still better.
—Yiddish proverb

One way we create meaning in our lives and our relationships is by demarcating space. We recognize certain places as the most desirable or preferred places for specific activities. We cherish other places for the sensations or experiences they've afforded us in the past, as individuals or as members of a collective. We keep mental lists of places we would like to have the chance to see or to live in. No matter how much or how little attention we tend to pay to space, we have come to treat certain spaces differently, either consciously or unconsciously. Among these is our home.

For our ancestors, the place of greatest meaning was the Temple *(Mikdash)* in Jerusalem. The Temple was maintained through special rituals, and its distinctive character was acknowledged through a highly choreographed dedication ceremony. The Rabbis teach us that our home is a *mikdash m'at,* a small sanctuary. Like the Temple, it is a place where our most cherished relationships and values can find rest and respect. It can be a sanctuary where we regroup before reengaging with the broader world.

Is there anything that diminishes the sanctity of your home? Anything that has made it less than a safe haven, less than the place where you find peace, hope, or strength? Hanukkah may be an especially appropriate time of year for you to focus your time and attention on identifying and committing yourself to addressing some of these questions, either alone or with your partner.

Like the idols that defiled the Temple in the time of the Maccabees, is there something that needs to be removed from your *mikdash m'at?* Conversely, is there something that, like the oil lamps in the Temple, needs to be restored, replaced, or replenished? Perhaps there is a minor indoor repair or remodeling project you can begin. Changing small things, like taking down a picture that one of you once loved but neither of you cares about any more, can make a difference. Oftentimes, changes require no hammers or nails, just creative thinking and reorganization. Do you both like the temperature of your home? Do you have symbols of your commitment (a wedding contract, a picture of your wedding day) that you would like to display in your home?

Jews who wish to dedicate a new home or rededicate an old one do so by hanging a mezuzah during a ceremony known as *Hanukkat HaBayit,* dedication of the home. The mezuzah, which contains verses of Torah, hangs on the doorpost to symbolize the home's special status and reminds the inhabitants of their responsibility to ensure that the space reflects their values. Whether you have just moved into a new home or made changes in the home you have, you might want to dedicate your space either by putting up a mezuzah for the first time, or reaffixing one you already have. You can invite others to join you or make it a ritual for just the two of you. Traditionally, we say the following prayer as we affix a mezuzah to the doorpost: *Barukh atah Adonai, Eloheinu Melekh haolam, asher kidshanu b'mitzvotav v'tzivanu likboa mezuzah;* We praise you, God, Source of Life, who makes us holy with your mitzvot and commands us to hang a mezuzah. We follow it with *Sheheheyanu* (see page 14).

Terri and Marilyn could not believe how quickly they had moved to Seattle. Within a month of Marilyn's new job offer, Terri's firm approved a transfer, they sold their condo in New York, bought a new home, said good-byes, and flew across the country. Before their furniture arrived in the van, they hung their mezuzah on the doorpost and spoke to each other about their dreams and prayers for this new space they would share. Later, when they had made connections in their new community, they filled their house with friends and neighbors for a celebration of *Hanukkat HaBayit.*

Fern and Chris came home one night to find their house had been broken into; everything had been trashed. After their initial cleanup, they decided to invite friends over to help them rededicate their home. Following a Native American custom, they went from room to room with burning sage to purify the space. Their friends' children paraded around the house clanging loudly on pots and pans, recalling a medieval Jewish practice for scaring away demons. Then they hung a brand-new mezuzah on the front doorpost and celebrated their newly sanctified space.

Hanging a mezuzah can have special significance reaching beyond affirming the sanctity of a home. A mezuzah hangs neither vertically nor horizontally, but on a slant. As with so many Jewish customs, the story of this one is tied to a story about a dispute. Jews living in different parts of the world read the Torah in different ways. Those in Spain and the Middle East read from a scroll propped up vertically; those in Germany and Eastern Europe read from one laid down on a table horizontally. Each group felt the orientation of the mezuzah should reflect the position of the Torah scroll in the synagogue. Eventually, the Rabbis came to a compromise consensus: A mezuzah should hang on a slant on the doorpost. As you enter your home, a mezuzah can remind you both that your home can be a holy space and that your ability to compromise with each other is an intrinsic part of that holiness.

Private and Public Space

The sanctity of our homes depends on our ability to find mutually acceptable ways for two people to feel safe, comfortable, and honored. That comfort also depends on the boundary between private and public space. The Talmud teaches that Jews should place their Hanukkah menorah in a window for the world to see (*Shabbat* 24a). This highlights an ongoing concern about what constitutes public and private space.

In our personal lives it takes time to determine which spaces are which and for whom a space may be private, semiprivate, or public. The look and feel of the public spaces in your home may be of primary importance for one of you, yet completely irrelevant for the other. You may not even define *comfortable, clean, messy, utilitarian, necessary,* or *aesthetic* in the same way, and the importance of these concepts for each of you is probably different as well. Are you in need of a novel way of looking at these differences, in need of working out a compromise position? Or are they issues that will never be resolved—and both of you can live with that?

Outside your home you also deal with issues related to boundaries between public and private. Consciously or unconsciously, you regularly make decisions about the ways you acknowledge your relationship in public. Are you both comfortable with how you express your closeness, your bonds with each other? Do certain displays of affection make one of you uncomfortable? Is there consistency in the way you treat each other in private and in public? Do you want there to be? Perhaps this is an area for you to begin introducing some small but meaningful changes.

Jewish tradition teaches that even when we are within the walls of our home, our personal sanctuary, we need to remember our connection with the larger world. There is an old Jewish custom of leaving a small part of a wall or ceiling in a home unpainted. Traditionally, this served as a visual reminder of the destruction of the Temple—and, by extension, of all the things in our world that are broken or missing or incomplete. Pauline Wengeroff, a nineteenth-century Lithuanian Jew, recalled a variation of this custom: In her childhood home there was a large black square painted on the red wallpaper with Hebrew words meaning "In memory of the destruction."

Each of us has a responsibility to move beyond our own safe space and do what we can to fix what is wrong in the larger community. The contemporary Jewish term for this is *tikkun olam*, repair of the world. How do we want to symbolically represent in our homes what needs repairing? Some families display boxes for collecting *tzedakah*, righteous giving. The custom Ari and Brenda developed was to put the change from their pockets on a plate on the kitchen table each night. Every morning they took the change with them to distribute to needy individuals they encountered on their way to work. What will be your nonverbal cue to get out into the world and do something to repair it? If you decide to rededicate your space so that it can better nurture the holiness of your relationship, you can create or dedicate an "unfinished" spot in your home to remind you of the work that is waiting to be done.

Almost everyone likes to receive gifts, and most of us get pleasure out of giving them as well. The national December shopping spree, however, often threatens to submerge the holidays themselves in a swell of materialism. In an effort to adapt to the Christmas season, many American Jews have made H̲anukkah into an occasion for giving elaborate and numerous gifts, especially to children. Many couples wonder how they can acknowledge the power of giving while disengaging from the commercial frenzy.

Jason and Stu long ago concluded that they were not interested in buying each other more "things." Since they both have holidays from work on Christmas Day, they make December 25 their charitable gift day. They discuss the state of the world and how best to express their shared values through their donations. They also explore with each other how they can honor their individual priorities when they disagree. They assess how much of their giving should go to Jewish causes, how much to universal concerns, how much to salving open wounds, and how much to systemic social change. They are acutely aware of how lucky they are to be in a position to share their good fortune with others. With a sense of gratitude and purpose they write each check, knowing that it represents their hope and commitment to making the world just a bit better in the coming year. This is their way of putting into action the H̲anukkah message: A little bit of oil can have a miraculous impact.

Celebrations/*Minhagim*

There is a beautiful traditional blessing for acknowledging and expressing appreciation for something new—anything from a new piece of clothing to a new season or holiday. Known as *Sheheh̲eyanu*, this blessing thanks the Source of Life for keeping us alive, sustaining us and allowing us to be here at this moment (see page 14). It is one of the blessings recited on the first day of Hanukkah, as well as at the start of other holidays and special moments during the year. Consider saying this blessing before you begin any ritual that is new to you, whether it is a ritual you have just invented or one you are just starting to perform.

Tradition says that we should light eight candles over the eight nights of Hanukkah, but how do we do it? According to the Talmud, "The House of Shammai made a ruling: On the first day of Hanukkah, we light eight candles; each day thereafter, we diminish the lights by one. The House of Hillel made a ruling: On the first day of Hanukkah, we light one candle; each day thereafter, we increase the lights by one" (Shabbat 21a).

Though Hillel's ruling became normative, you can try lighting the candles both ways. Discuss which one gives you a greater feeling of hope. Discuss compromises and new ways of doing things you've explored during the past year.

The second blessing traditionally said over the Hanukkah candles recalls the miracles done "for our ancestors in those days" (see page 14).

- Share a story with your partner, from Jewish history or your personal histories, that you consider a miracle.

- Take time to speak with your partner about something enduring in your relationship that you continue to marvel at—something that lasts, like the single cruse of oil in the Temple.

Think about your home, and the possible meaning and use a mezuzah could have for you.

- Take a moment to articulate the ways in which you have made, or would like to make, your home more holy.

- If you already have a mezuzah, take a look at it. If it needs cleaning, give it a little attention. Are there other rooms in your house that you might want to dedicate with a mezuzah on the doorpost?

- If you have never hung a mezuzah, look into doing so. There are styles to suit all tastes and budgets.

- When you buy a mezuzah, the decorative outer case does not include the inner scroll, which you have to purchase separately. Although the traditional scroll contains Bible verses written on parchment by a trained scribe, consider composing and writing your own text for your mezuzah.

Revisit the past. Retell your personal stories.

- Make a holiday pilgrimage to the homes you lived in as children, and tell each other stories about your past. If distance precludes a trip, substitute old movies, slides, or photos—but don't skip the stories!

- Do the same with the homes you've shared.

Learning with a Partner/Hevruta

For every human being there rises
A light that reaches straight to heaven.
And when two souls that are destined to be together
Find each other, their streams of light flow together,
And a single brighter light goes forth from their
united being.

—Baal Shem Tov

Once the realization is accepted that even between
the closest human beings infinite distances continue
to exist, a wonderful living side by side can grow up,
if they succeed in loving the distance between them

which makes it possible for each to see the other
whole and against a wide sky.

—Rainier Maria Rilke

Questions for Discussion

1. How do these descriptions of relationship resonate with you?

2. Which of these images comes closest to describing your current relationship?

3. Which of these images is more compelling to you?

4. What images and metaphors approximate your ideal relationship?

This house displays our virtue to each other.
I swept the kitchen floor twice this week.
But I took the trash to the dump Tuesday.
I am putting up shelves, so kiss me.
See how the freshly polished table shines
like a red, red apple with love.

—Marge Piercy

Questions for Discussion

1. How do you "display your virtue" to each other through the tasks of keeping and maintaining your home?

2. In a spirit of giving, do you want to make some changes in how these tasks are done?

3. What shines in your home "like a red, red apple with love"?

*By wisdom a house is built, and by understanding it
is moored. By knowledge the rooms are filled with
all precious and pleasant treasure.*

—**Proverbs 24:3–4**

Questions for Discussion

1. What are the precious and pleasant treasures in your home?

2. What enables you to recognize your dwelling place as your home?

3. What makes it special or sacred?

Reaching Out/*Gemilut* <u>*Hesed*</u>

If neither of you observes Christmas, give the gift of yourself by volunteering at a hospital or nursing home on Christmas Day, so that staff who celebrate the holiday can be relieved of their duties.

Some couples do their charitable giving at the end of the calendar year. Find a time when the two of you can do yours together.

Buy or make for your partner something that your partner will feel enhances your home.

Begin preserving the story of your family. Interview the oldest living relatives in your clan, and ask them to tell you the stories as far back as they can recall. Record these stories and offer them as gifts. The older members will be thrilled to have their narratives preserved, and the younger ones will appreciate them someday.

Purim

Purim, a late winter holiday, means "lots," as in "drawing lots," an ancient symbol for chance and fortune. The Purim tale recounted in the Book of Esther relates an unanticipated reversal of fortune. The tone is one of parody and farce, though the topic is deadly serious. The king of Persia orders the annihilation of the Jews after his advisor Haman convinces him, based on one Jew's refusal to bow down to him, that all Jews are disloyal. That Jew, Mordecai, has a niece, Esther, who is one of the king's wives. To save her people, Esther invites the king and Haman to a banquet and reveals herself as a Jew. Angry at Haman's treachery, the king issues a new decree: The Jews can both defend themselves and avenge their losses. The Jews survive; the king keeps his Jewish wife, hangs Haman, and makes Mordecai his primary advisor.

While *Megillat Esther*, the Scroll of Esther, popularly known as "the *Megillah*," is being read aloud in the synagogue, Jews customarily "blot out" the name of Haman, their nemesis, with shouts and mechanical noisemakers (*graggers* in Yiddish) whenever his name is mentioned. We stage humorous plays and skits (*Purim-shpiels* in Yiddish), most often parodies of those in power. We give food and donations to the poor (*matanot l'evy-onim*) and send packages of food to friends and neighbors (*mishloach manot*).

CHAPTER TWO

Playing, Laughing, and Taking Risks: Purim

Our sincerest laughter
With some pain is fraught ...

—**Percy Bysshe Shelley**

Make noise, make lots of noise! Let yourself have a really good time! Social conventions are suspended! Be playful, relax, and laugh! This is how we are told to celebrate Purim.

What a wonderful way to break the gloom of late winter. Some of you may have memories of dressing up, of going to or participating in *Purim-shpiels*. You may recall sitting in the synagogue, which is a place of seriousness and decorum the rest of the year, and being invited, in fact expected, to react boisterously to the reading of the *Megillah*.

The Jewish holiday cycle offers many stories of grave threats to the Jews, even near-annihilation. On some occasions we cry. On some we reflect. But on Purim we laugh. The terror of the *Megillah*'s story is tempered with humor and irony. It encourages us to laugh at ourselves and our world, to appreciate life's fundamental absurdity. Purim reminds us that we need to take risks, as well as create or take advantage of opportunities for celebration whenever we can.

Playing and Laughing

We all have fond memories of playful moments, laughter, and abandon. That time when you and your best friend painted each other's faces and walked into the school library.... That summer your bunk adopted a crayfish, named it, fed it, and wrote songs about it.... That evening when the elevator door opened to let someone on while you and your beloved were singing and whirling each other around in a waltz.... Just remembering these moments can still bring a smile to your face, take you out of time and away from your daily pressures, and reconnect you to your playful side.

You and your partner have found ways to play with each other—through formal games, wordplays, jokes, fantasies, dressing up, running in the waves, hot-dogging on the slopes. Whether planned or spontaneous, playing can help you maintain an intimate relationship. And it can be a central part of your shared physical intimacy as well.

Joan was always surprised to see how thoroughly Sid enjoyed watching *The Three Stooges*. It seemed so infantile to her! Most of the time Sid's humor was wry and sophisticated. But when given a moment with those three idiots, he'd belly-laugh as he rarely did otherwise. He couldn't explain why they tickled him so, but they did. Joan came to understand these moments as glimpses of Sid as he must have been as a child, and to love them.

Humor is tricky. You think your sense of humor is in sync with someone else's, and then you find he is left unmoved by something you found hilarious. Or an ironic premise that brings a broad appreciative smile to your face means nothing to your partner, who's left scratching her head, bemused and stymied by your reaction.

Real laughter is a spontaneous release of emotion, a true and raw expression of feelings from within. Laughing can be triggered by an overwhelming sense of joy and abandon; it can also be triggered by a sense of discomfort and conflict. The things that make us laugh often indicate the sources of our deepest pain, our darkest fears. Many of us use humor as a defense against hurt. Through the guise of parody, irony, and sarcasm, we can make light of deep fears and gain mastery over them, at least momentarily. So it is in the topsy-turvy world of Queen Esther and the *Megillah*.

Each of us also has our demons. Each of us knows people and situations that frighten us so profoundly that we are unable to engage with others and the world in our characteristic ways. But we hope that, like later generations of Jews recalling the story of Esther, we will ultimately be able to laugh at the things that once frightened us.

When Marsha and Hal pulled out an old photo album, they came across a picture from their fifth anniversary. There they were, standing in front of a hotel with plastered smiles on their faces, "making nice" for the camera. They came back telling everyone they'd had a wonderful time, but the truth was it had been a miserable attempt at a tryst. Marsha felt that her dreams of romance had been brushed aside when Hal approached her with wild abandon, thrilled that there were no kids in sight. They'd bickered all weekend long, and they came home grumpier than when they'd left. This year, though, the sight of the picture brought a smile to Marsha's face. She began to laugh and said, "I was so unaware of how inhibited the kids made you feel back then. I'm glad you eventually got over that."

Hal began to laugh too. "Yeah, just in time for them to know what the noises meant!" He continued, "And I finally got it that the romancing wasn't to turn *me* on. Duh—it was to make you feel good about yourself. We missed so much back then."

Another important part of having fun with our partners is using fantasy. Purim, more than any other holiday, reminds us how vital it is to let our imaginations run wild. An orphaned girl, a member of a religious minority, becomes the queen of a vast empire by being chosen in a beauty pageant? A government gives Jews permission to take vengeance against those who sought to destroy them? Could these things really have happened? In all likelihood, no. But playing with such possibilities can be very powerful. For centuries, one day a year, that's just what Jews have done.

Sex, love, power, and violence. We can relate to these urges and the fantasies they engender, because we all have experienced them. But do we have opportunities to share them with anyone? Do we acknowledge them as fantasies and allow ourselves to share them and then laugh at them? Many couples find that letting each other in on their fantasies—be they sexual, social, political, or economic—deepens their relationship and adds a dimension to the ways that they relax and play with each other. Sharing our fantasies with our partners, however, can be risky. Before we share, we need to consider our partner's personal fears and insecurities and see if our fantasies might tap into them. The last thing we want is for our attempt to draw nearer to result in our partner's being hurt or pushed away.

Whenever Rick had a rough day, he'd come home and weave a fanciful tale for himself and Stephanie. One night he spoke at length about how his overbearing boss had turned into a hot-air balloon and floated off—out of the office, beyond the building, past the city limits, and out of sight. Another time, he told about how his inept secretary had been transformed into a polite and efficient female robot who arrived one morning with a completely revised, magnificently laid-out annual report, asking what else needed to be done! By the time he finished, they were both laughing hysterically at the fantasies they knew would never come true. The stories had no chance of changing reality, but they invariably helped them both focus on his frustrations in a playful and cathartic way.

Taking Risks: Hiding and Revealing

I am what I am
And what I am is an illusion.

—Jerry Herman

To laugh is to take a risk: a risk that by sharing your laughter you are revealing, directly or indirectly, something hidden about yourself; a risk that whether or not your humor is shared, your revelation will be honored and treated with care. But we take risks all the time, most often without depending on humor to shield us. When you decided to set out on a life path together, you, too, were taking a risk, probably the biggest one of your lives—intending, on faith, to use a positive past and present as the foundation for a largely unknown future.

The ancient Jewish tradition of a groom's lifting the bride's veil to ensure that he is marrying the correct woman often makes us laugh.

We are amused by the prospect of someone's unwittingly marrying the wrong person. We laugh too because we know that even if we marry the person we

The origin of this custom is attributed to Jacob's mistaken acceptance of Leah for Rachel in Genesis 29. To ensure that a groom has the right bride, customs related to veiling or unveiling the bride prior to the ceremony became part of traditional Jewish wedding rituals.

expect to marry, there are veils upon veils within our relation-ship still to be lifted. We will lift some of our own, revealing something new to our partners. Our partners will lift some of ours, whether or not we are ready.

Much to our ongoing surprise, we've learned that with each new circumstance, we can discover something new about how a partner views, experiences, and responds to the world. For every-thing we know about this person, there are countless things we don't know or, as is sometimes the case, we think we'd rather not know. Sometimes we find ourselves wondering whether we committed to the wrong person after all!

Michelle was hyperorganized. She would plan for things well in advance and always finished projects ahead of schedule. Don had come to adore this particular trait of Michelle's. She laid out the road map of the day or weekend or vacation, and he would happily join her in what was planned. He hadn't realized how much he'd come to depend on her operating this way until Michelle's dad had a major stroke. Don had answered the phone, and when he told Michelle she became paralyzed. He asked her what she wanted to do, but she had no idea, no plan. She just sat down on the couch and stared into space. Don said, "I'm going to book us a flight to Florida as soon as possible." She looked at him blankly and nodded in agreement. He suggested she go up-stairs and pack. She just sat there numbly. These were new cir-cumstances for both of them, and they were experiencing unfamiliar sides of themselves and each other.

While extraordinary circumstances can bring to the fore as-pects of our personalities that are not normally present, our daily interactions often offer us opportunities to choose which parts of ourselves we wish to reveal. Sometimes we pay attention and go along with social convention. Sometimes we consider our own comfort and the comfort of the person we're speaking to. At other times we consciously choose to hide what we fear will keep us from achieving our desired ends. Then, like Esther's hiding her Jewishness, we choose not to reveal an essential part of our selves.

Think back to when you first met; remember the things you immediately let your spouse know about you. Now remember the things you consciously tried to hide. Someone or something told you these were wise choices. And perhaps at the time, they were.

Allison was relaxed and comfortable when she met Bob. They had an easy time finding things to talk about. They both liked foreign movies; they both had close friends from childhood. They joked about the similarities they saw in their bosses. But when he brought up his family, telling loving anecdotes about his relationship with his father and brothers, Allison felt herself becoming anxious. Her family's time and energy always had focused on her mother, who was mentally ill. In the past when she had shared this, too many people had reacted negatively. And, as her father had always told her, it was nobody's business but theirs, anyway. And so she shared her only heartwarming childhood memory, not letting on that it was one of a kind. Large or small, the things we choose not to reveal demonstrate our sense of insecurity, our areas of greatest vulnerability.

As the *Megillah* tells us, Esther slid by for quite a while as queen without ever revealing her Jewishness. Only when faced with the threat of her people's annihilation did she finally take action, heeding Mordecai's words:

> Do not imagine that you, of all the Jews, will escape with your life by being in the king's palace. On the contrary, if you keep silent in this crisis, relief and deliverance will come to the Jews from another quarter, while you and your father's house will perish. And who knows, perhaps you have attained a royal position for just such a crisis.
>
> —*Esther 4:13–14*

Think of the times you have contemplated telling your partner something, and hesitated. Like Esther, there was some question in your mind. Did you expect, as the *Megillah* put it, to "find favor" in your spouse's sight, enough favor to expect a loving response? Recall how you tried to postpone that moment and how eventually you realized you were ready for the revelation (if you ever were).

When Bill's grandfather died, he and Cathy inherited money that had long been in the family. Bill was aware that his ancestors had originally settled in the American South in the early nineteenth century, but he knew little about them. While the will was in probate, he began to investigate and found to his dismay that his ancestors had been slaveholders. Both he and Cathy had long wanted to pay back their debts and put some money away for their retirement, and Cathy had begun to talk about how they could now do it, but Bill felt that because of the origins of the money, it was not theirs to spend on themselves. The night before the will was settled, he sat with Cathy and told her that he wanted to use the money to set up scholarships for African-American students. He knew in his heart that this was what he needed to do, even if Cathy objected.

Sometimes self-revelation is not only a personal but also a political act of courage, a risk we take for the sake of social justice. You and your partner may not see eye to eye on all political issues; however, Jewish tradition encourages you to actively demonstrate your concern for the world. Both the Torah and later Jewish writings describe our obligation to recognize, speak out against, and fight social, economic, and political injustices. We all face the same questions that confronted Queen Esther: when and how to act within the system (as Esther did when she married the king) and when and how to take a stand outside the system (as Esther did when she revealed her identity as a Jew), even if it might lead to rejection.

We put on masks at Purim both to hide and to reveal. A pair of wordplays in Hebrew makes this point: The Hebrew root of Esther's name is connected to the word *hester*, which means "hidden." And the word *Megillah* can be rendered as *m'galeh*, which means "revealed." Thus, by reading the *Megillah*, what was hidden is revealed! By listening for what's behind your partner's silences, hesitations, laughter, or tears, you can learn to hear what your partner is hiding. Your partner, feeling better understood, may learn to respond to you in the same way, thus allowing you to risk revealing your hidden fears.

The Book of Esther is the only biblical book that does not mention God. But some Rabbis say that God is not absent, merely hidden. They suggest that precisely when the Jews of Persia needed God's help, it was available through human action, not a miraculous divine intervention. The story of Purim reminds us to consider the possibility that what we fear is missing may actually be present in some unexpected form. There are times when our partners are offering us the love, companionship, encouragement, or hope we need and crave, but they are doing it in a manner we do not expect or interpret correctly. If we look at what we *are* receiving, rather than what we think we are *not* receiving, we and our partners can develop a deeper sense of appreciation for each other.

Couples come together for many different reasons: companionship, sexual attraction, family pressure, money, power, and shared dreams and hopes. Over time our reasons for remaining together may change, but we rarely take time to acknowledge this process or how it has affected our sense of shared purpose. In the Book of Esther, after dismissing a disobedient wife, the king looks for a queen who will accept his authority and publicly affirm his high status and importance. Esther agrees to take on this role. When she eventually approaches the king, asking him to accede to *her* needs and wishes, she doesn't know if he will be willing or able to change the whole nature of their relationship. She wonders if their relationship is strong enough to survive even if their way of relating to each other changes.

Rhoda and Tammy met and fell in love during college when they both volunteered for the Big Sister Program. Their most intense bond developed around their shared struggle with their families, who could not honor their relationship. The pain of those early years still lingered even though now, almost two decades later, both their families and the world had changed. Their relationship was no longer dependent on their presenting a united front against a hostile world. They delighted in the knowledge that their shared "cause" had shifted, from defending their right to love, to supporting each other's professional endeavors and long-term goals.

When and How We Celebrate

> And so, on the thirteenth day of the twelfth month—that is, the month of Adar—when the king's command and decree were to be executed … the Jews mustered in their cities to attack those who sought their hurt … and the Jews in Shushan mustered again on the fourteenth day of Adar.... The rest of the Jews, those in the king's provinces … rested on the fourteenth day and made it a day of feasting and merrymaking. (But the Jews of Shushan mustered on both the thirteenth and fourteenth days, and so rested on the fifteenth, and made it a day of feasting and merrymaking.)
>
> —*Esther 9:1–18*

The Book of Esther acknowledges that Jews in different places celebrated the same occasion on different days and through different rituals. We make choices, consciously or unconsciously, about how and when to relax, play, or celebrate, taking into account physical factors, social context, and timing. Most important, we consider what it is that we seek to achieve. But members of a couple often find that although they agree about the broad brush strokes, they disagree about the details.

One night over dinner, Lester and Mitch were discussing their upcoming anniversary. It would be their twenty-fifth, and they agreed that it would be fun to have a party. They pulled out their calendars to figure out a time. The Sunday immediately following their anniversary was open, and they penciled it in. Then Lester asked: "What time should we have everyone come over?"

"Come over?" Mitch countered. "I was thinking of renting a place and going all out."

And so their focus shifted to the "how" of celebrating. There wouldn't be a party unless they could find a way to celebrate that appealed to both of them.

The biblical tale of Esther offers an additional insight into the options we have when we celebrate: We can focus solely on ourselves; or we can share our joy and good fortune with others. At Purim, we are told our celebration is not complete unless we reach out to those less fortunate by giving gifts to the poor, and sending out portions of food to friends and acquaintances. Our personal and collective memories can motivate us to contribute constructively to the world whenever we celebrate.

For as long as they could remember, Selma and Henry had celebrated their friend Adam's birthday with him. When Adam was killed by a drunk driver, Selma and Henry dreaded the first birthday without him. They had spent weeks each year selecting the perfect gift for Adam. This year, the gift wouldn't be for him, it would be in his memory. They talked a long time before deciding to make a donation to Mothers Against Drunk Driving.

Jim had memories of visiting his kid brother in the hospital while he was undergoing rounds of chemotherapy. No day in the hospital was easy, but the holidays were especially tough. Years later Jim and his wife, Sharon, decided to visit the local children's hospital around Purim, dressed as clowns. This way they'd take the playfulness prescribed by the holiday to a new and different level, dressing up and clowning around with each other while entertaining some hospitalized kids in the process. Jim's unpleasant memories were converted into a celebratory act, just as Purim takes a painful story and caps it off with gestures to heal the world.

There is a Jewish joke that made the rounds a while ago. "Jewish holidays can be summed up in three simple sentences: They tried to kill us. We survived. Let's eat." Like many jokes, this one has a lot of truth to it, and Purim certainly fits the bill.

Historically, in addition to celebrating Purim itself at the end of winter, some Jewish communities declared a *Purim Katan* (literally, "Little Purim") to celebrate their own community's continued survival following a time when its existence was threatened. The Jews of Frankfurt-am-Main, Germany, celebrated their *Purim Katan* on the twentieth of Adar, to mark the execution of the chief anti-Semite and the readmission of Jews to their town in 1616. The Jews of Tiberias celebrated a *Purim Katan* on the seventh of Elul, dating from 1743 when they were saved from impending war with neighboring Arab countries. The Jews of Casablanca declared the second of Kislev their *Purim Katan* to commemorate their being saved from anti-Jewish riots and Nazi occupation in 1943.

Not only communities encounter threats and survive them. In your personal lives you have undoubtedly experienced moments when you were acutely aware of your own physical vulnerability. And in your life as a couple, you have probably lived through periods when your stability, your sense of security, or your hope for a future was compromised or significantly threatened. You may also recall the series of interactions or events that signaled for you the passing of that threat and the continuation of life, however altered.

Perhaps it was a serious illness, a financial reversal, the death of a beloved relative or friend, an affair, or a physical attack. Looking back and acknowledging the emotions of the time and rejoicing in your continued life together can be a source of strength, comfort, and joy. Either on Purim itself or on some other significant day, you can celebrate your own *Purim Katan* complete with telling your story, expressing anger and fear (perhaps using a *gragger* at the mention of whatever represented the threat), and finally reveling in the fact that you are still here to celebrate together.

Celebrations/*Minhagim*

Take out your calendars and choose a date in the near future as a play day. (You could, in fact, plan your play day for Purim itself.) Be faithful about not scheduling anything else on that day.

- Decide now how you will use the time … OR

- Do something on the spur of the moment on that date.

Plan for an evening or afternoon of laughter.

- Choose a funny movie, play, comedian, or book to enjoy together.

- When the time arrives, put out your favorite snacks.

- Get into something comfortable.

- Relax and enjoy!

Jewish tradition teaches that, like the Torah, every person has seventy faces.

- Make masks out of papier-mâché or clay or paper and paints or markers.

- Make some of your own faces and some of your partner's.

- Talk about the different faces each of you has.

- Play with the masks and have fun.

- Save the masks to pull on during a fight (sometimes laughing at yourselves can break the negative energy).

If there has been some reversal of fortune in your own lives in the past, consider declaring the date as your personal *Purim Katan.* On that date, take out a photo, a bill, a book, or another item that you clearly associate with that time of intensified vulnerability.

- Look at the item and recall memories related to that time.

- Drown out the narrative with noisemakers or loud sounds whenever the threat is mentioned.

- Discuss what it's like to be where you are now.

- Discuss the blessing of time that offers you an opportunity to now reflect and celebrate.

- Offer words of gratitude and prayer that you have survived the threat.

Learning with a Partner/_Hevruta_

Each of you select a video of one of your favorite comedies and watch them.

Questions for Discussion

1. What was the funniest part of the movie for you?

2. Which moments of the movie didn't work for you?

3. What did you learn about your partner by watching him/her react to the movies?

4. What did you learn about yourself?

When Rabbi Eleazar of Kosnitz, son of Rabbi Moshe, son of the Maggid of Kosnitz, was young, he was a guest in the house of Rabbi Naftali of Ropshitz. They were standing in a room where the curtains had been drawn, and he looked at them with surprise. When his host asked him the cause of his surprise, he said, "If you want people to look in, why the curtain? If you don't, why the window?"

Rabbi Naftali then said, "And what is the answer, do you think?"

"When you want someone you love to look in," said the young rabbi, "you draw aside the curtain."

—Hasidic tale as told by Chaim Stern

Questions for Discussion

1. What did you originally feel you needed to hide from your partner?

2. What changed in you or your partner or the world that enabled you to reveal it?

3. What is something you've come to know about your partner during the past year that you were either not aware of or not attuned to before?

4. Is there something you'd like to reveal to your partner now? Perhaps it's time to take the risk.

My dear Cristina, one must not be obsessed with the idea of security, even the security of one's own virtue. Spiritual life is not compatible with security. To save oneself one has to take risks.

—Ignazio Silone

Questions for Discussion

1. Does this idea resonate with you?

2. What risks that have reflected your spiritual life have you taken, at the risk of your own security?

3. How might your partner help you take a risk you've been afraid to take?

Reaching Out/*Gemilut Hesed*

Bring a moment of joy and light to someone who is institutionalized or homebound—play an instrument, sing, read a book, cook, redecorate.

Find a reason to celebrate with your coworkers; bring your partner along and prepare something festive to eat.

Take the time, with your partner, to contact someone who is important to the two of you, and let them know what they mean to you and how grateful you are that they are part of your life.

Choose a time when you are rejoicing, Purim or some other date, and take a moment to remember those less fortunate:

- Write a check to an organization that works with the poor in your area.

- Buy or prepare extra food to donate the next time you plan a party or invite guests over for a meal.

Volunteer with an organization that is working to change society so that people no longer need to hide aspects of their identities (religion, gender, age, sexual orientation, ethnicity) to avoid discrimination.

Support the work of a group that helps people who experience a threat similar to one that you have gone through, by donating money or time to a cancer society, twelve-step program, marriage retreat center, or the like.

Pesah

Pesah (usually translated "Passover") is a weeklong spring festival celebrating the Jews' liberation from Egyptian slavery and the rebirth of the natural world. The seder at Pesah provides an annual gathering for extended families and is frequently an opportunity for Jews to open their homes to guests.

For the week of Pesah, Jews refrain from eating _hameitz,_ leaven. Traditionally, we remove breads (and other foods that rise when cooked) from our homes, often leading to an arduous spring cleaning. We eat matzah, the "bread of affliction," which helps us recall the hasty flight of the Israelites from Egypt. Similarly, at the seder, a celebratory meal, we eat bitter herbs (usually horseradish) to remember the bitterness of slavery, and _haroset,_ a sweet fruit-and-nut mixture, an edible metaphor for the hope of freedom.

A book known as the Haggadah (telling) leads participants through the prescribed rituals. Biblical, rabbinic, and contemporary stories, songs, and rituals dramatize the Jewish journey from slavery to liberation. Modern Haggadot often relate the ancient story to universal themes of personal and communal freedom as well. Favorite seder rituals: The children ask the Four Questions, which prompts the storytelling; they search for the _afikoman,_ a hidden piece of matzah, to end the seder; and they open the door for the invisible guest, Elijah the Prophet, who, it is said, will be the harbinger of a healed world.

CHAPTER THREE

Coming Home, Finding Freedom: Pesa<u>h</u>

We spent the night recounting
Far-off events full of wonder,
And because of all the wine
The mountains will skip like rams.
Tonight they exchange questions:
The wise, the godless, the simple-minded and the
    child.
And time reverses its course,
Today flowing back into yesterday,
Like a river enclosed at its mouth.
Each of us has been a slave in Egypt,
Soaked straw and clay with sweat,
And crossed the sea dry-footed.
You too, stranger.
This year in fear and shame,
Next year in virtue and justice.

                               —Primo Levi

Exodus 12 recounts the scene: The Israelites are told to take "a lamb for each family" and eat the flesh with unleavened bread and bitter herbs (Exodus 12:4, 8, 11). This first "seder" takes place the night before the Israelites leave Egypt. The next day, before the escaping slaves have even made it across the Red Sea, the instructions for the future are given: "Remember this day on which you went free.... Seven days you shall eat unleavened bread.... And you shall explain it to your son" (Exodus 13:6, 8). Before the liberation is complete, plans are being made to remember it! From the very beginning the great themes of the holiday of Pesah are already in place: the gathering of the tribe, the relationship between freedom and law, and the power of hope in the promise of the future.

Coming Home: The Gathering of the Tribe

In American culture, national communal ritual still exists, but it is thin. Thanksgiving is one ritual that endures. The rites are simple: The tribe gathers; turkey is consumed. For many families additional routines and customs have developed: watching football or the parade on television, competing over who has the worst traffic story, eating a particular turkey leftover dish the next day. One creative Jewish family, in a bit of cross-cultural sharing, hides the wishbone after dinner and gives a prize to the child who finds it.

Families sometimes tell the story of the brave Pilgrims and helpful Indians many of us learned in grade school, but this is usually brief. That myth has been "broken" for many of us, replaced by a more morally ambiguous story of the Europeans' conquering and displacing the Native Americans. Yet the core value, deep and humble gratitude for the blessing of food and of being an American, is still salient. And beyond that, at the deepest level of meaning, is the gathering of the tribe, the family reunion, the celebration (ambivalence included) of our ties to the ones to whom we are related.

Like Thanksgiving, Pesa<u>h</u> is a contemporary pilgrimage for Jewish families. Unlike Thanksgiving, the script handed down by tradition is long and detailed, the specifics of table setting and food elaborate. The rituals are complex. While the original myth of God freeing the Jews from Egypt with a mighty hand may no longer be believed literally, the story still resonates powerfully. Within memory, Jews have been on the move from one place to another; the image of a group of slaves triumphing over an evil empire continues to inspire. It is no wonder that Pesa<u>h</u> is still observed even after so many other Jewish practices have been abandoned.

The gathering of the tribe is central to the meaning of the seder. This has been true since the very beginning. So here we are, over three thousand years later, gathering as families to explain it all to the next generation. No matter with whom we end up having a seder, this holiday reminds us that we are links in generational chains. In certain ways Pesa<u>h</u> is always with one's entire family—the family members who are at the table, the family members who choose not to come, the family members who are gone. In Europe before World War II, Jewish families sometimes prepared the seder table with full place settings for the relatives who had immigrated to America. Later, those American relatives set places for the ones who had stayed behind and were killed by the Nazis. Whether or not we set places for them at the table, the absent relatives are with us. And we are again the children we were when we asked the Four Questions from the Haggadah. It is a paradox: The holiday is about an exodus—leaving, going out, setting free. But we celebrate through an ingathering—going back, returning, uniting again with those from whom we came.

For a couple, the gathering of the clan (or the absence of a gathering) raises all the issues related to extended families. Where you both come from makes a difference in how the two of you make your life together. For better or worse, Pesah and the time leading up to the seder often provide an opportunity for those issues to emerge. For a non-Jew who marries into a Jewish family, there is the added task of fitting into a traditional event that is not your own tradition. But two Jews often have differences as well. Their families may compete for attention. Some couples must deal with Jewish families with very different modes of observance, others with families that present challenges quite separate from the holiday. Whether it is Pesah or some other time in the year, the goal for a couple is to hold onto themselves and their relationship during the emotional intensity of homecoming and tribe-gathering.

When performing a wedding, some rabbis make a point of noting that only the two people marrying each other should stand under the *huppah*, the wedding canopy. Some people believe the canopy represents the marital bed, and as such is the sacred space of these two individuals alone. Parents, siblings, and friends may gather around and offer support, but they should not be inside the precincts. The psychologist Judith Wallerstein wrote that the first task of any marriage is, figuratively, to build walls for the *huppah*. She adds that the walls should have gateways, but the couple should control the gates.

Of course, saying that is the easy part. When we choose our partners, we get an entire family, sometimes multiple families. In Nikos Kazantzakis's *Zorba the Greek,* the old man was asked, "Have you been married?" He replied, "Of course—wife, house, kids, the full catastrophe." These days, most of us live in nuclear families, not so closely tied on a day-to-day basis with the extended clan. On Pesah, however, it is often "the full catastrophe."

Carrie and Joe went food shopping a few nights before their seder. While pushing the cart through the aisles, they had a long talk about the challenges of the evening to come. They knew that their parents' holiday customs were very different, and always produced disagreements and tension when they got together. They agreed to help each other remain cool in the face of this. But things did not work out quite as they planned. As their parents argued over everything from which matzah to break to what the appropriate "prize" was for finding the *afikoman,* Joe and Carrie got more frazzled. They found themselves sniping at each other rather than being supportive; their supermarket resolution was long forgotten. By the end of the evening, they both felt they should be hunting for the *afikoman* along with the children.

Boundaries between the generations protect couples, but they are hard to maintain at these moments when families converge. These are times when couples need to be extra careful to keep their focus on their primary loyalty, each other. And they need to remember that they are adults, even when their parents are present. When there are blended families with multiple generations from multiple partnerships, this becomes even more crucial. While so much of the preparation for this holiday involves physical acts of cleaning, cooking, and setting up, for a couple the spiritual preparation for Pesa<u>h</u> may involve checking for cracks in their own foundation and vowing to seal them so negative energy from outside doesn't seep in.

Extending beyond the Tribe

Near the beginning of the Haggadah, we find the declaration: "May all who are hungry, come and eat. May all who are in need celebrate Pesa<u>h</u> with us." Some of us open our door at this point to symbolize the intention of this formulaic statement. Many of us make sure to have guests at the seder and feel a special pleasure in opening our homes at this time. Others share in the spirit of this call by hosting people at other times of the year. Jewish tradition prizes hospitality. It teaches that Abraham, the father of the Jewish people, kept his tent open on both sides, so wayfarers could enter from either direction. When couples share a commitment to hospitality, it can provide them with a rich connection to each other. But hospitality is not a simple matter for couples. How open do we each want our home to be, and do we each see it the same way?

Walter's first wife had grown up in a very private family and found it hard to let others into her home. Walter soon learned that bringing unannounced guests for dinner was not something to be done lightly. In his new marriage to Francine, he was thrilled to finally be able to indulge his own sense of a home as a place to welcome others. He and Francine discussed all this before they were married, and it was a shared value that gave them a great deal of joy. Over the years, however, some periods demanded new arrangements. When Francine went through a difficult time after losing a job, she discovered that she needed her home to be a sanctuary where she could count on finding only Walter. Later, things shifted back again.

Hospitality is not simply the intuitive notion of opening your space to friends and family, to people you like and with whom you enjoy sharing a meal or a celebration. The Haggadah is clear—*all* who are hungry should come and eat. In case we don't get the point, the Torah is quite specific in noting to whom we owe hospitality. The "stranger" is frequently mentioned. On Pesah, when we are reminded that as Jews we were once strangers in the land of Egypt, we are especially called to think about who the strangers in our midst are, and how we can most effectively offer them the hospitality they need.

Partners might also think about their own relationship in terms of the value of hospitality. Hospitality is about making room in your space for someone else. How are we hospitable to our own intimate partners? There are very tangible ways, such as preparing a meal when they are hungry or offering different kinds of sustenance when they are in need. But there is also the subtler kind of hospitality, simply letting them in, opening our own hearts in ways that allow them in. And here is where the command concerning the stranger becomes relevant. Sometimes we look at our partner and see someone we know well and love. Other times we see a new face, or one that we have seen before but have never fully understood. Sometimes, we look across the kitchen table at breakfast and wonder, "Who is this stranger?" This is when we need to cultivate hospitality. We need to try to let our partners in, even when they are most mysterious to us.

Finding Freedom: A Paradox

The rules for the seder are manifold and complex. Rabbis in Europe would postpone their own seders till late at night so that they would be available to answer legal questions that arose during their congregants' seders. The entire Pesaḥ holiday, from the removal of the leaven to the last day of the festival, is ordered and scripted, rules abounding. Does it seem paradoxical that the holiday with the most rules in the Jewish year is the one dedicated to freedom?

Perhaps. But it would not surprise Barry Schwartz, a Swarthmore College psychologist who has written about the "paradox of choice." Schwartz argues that we are drowning in opportunities to choose, and also to regret the options we have forsaken. These range from the simplest activities, such as selecting a pair of jeans, to the more complex matters of choosing a computer, a college, a vacation, or a medical treatment plan. Having too many options makes us more anxious and ultimately less content with our decisions. Schwartz suggests that, for the sake of our mental health, we need to limit our choices.

Ritual provides a set of limitations in which freedom can emerge. Once the Israelites were free of Pharaoh, the first law that was given to them as a group was to establish the month of the Exodus as the first month (see Exodus 12:1). It is not surprising that our first communal command is about the calendar. The calendar is a perfect example of a structure that liberates. The very fact that we commit ourselves to observing the seder on a particular night means we don't have to spend time deciding when we will do it. It's right there on the calendar. One less choice to make. What a relief.

We moderns cherish our autonomy. Yet it is precisely when we least feel like spontaneously doing something—for example, saying a blessing over food—that we probably need the rules most. This is where discipline and order come in.

In our relationships we often find that being completely free and unstructured is scary, and that rules, rituals, help us to feel safe and free in a different way. The most obvious example is the commitment to a monogamous relationship. For those who make that choice, all kinds of other choices are no longer on the table. One does not have to go into the world each day and decide, person by person, "Would I rather be with this one than with my partner?" The decision has been made; the limitation can be liberating.

Within marriage, rules and commitments support us. Amy believed her parents were naturally the most congenial couple on earth. Throughout her childhood she experienced them as loving and connected in a natural and seamless way. As an adult about to embark on a marriage of her own, she asked her parents how they had gotten so lucky. It turned out that luck was only part of it. Amy's parents had quite a number of rules unknown to Amy that invisibly structured their time together so that it worked well. For instance, Amy's parents told her that in the early days of their marriage they had quickly learned that neither of them was at all pleasant to be with in the early morning. "For fifty years, we enforced a strict rule: No words are exchanged before breakfast," they told her. Amy was amazed. She had never even noticed!

Other couples develop their own rules that provide them with the order they need for their lives to flow graciously: "Never go to bed angry." "Call each other once a day." "Always say, 'Good dinner' no matter what."

Preparing for Sacred Time

An old joke tells of a rabbi and rebbetzin who were wrongly imprisoned in Russia under the czar and were offered their freedom just two weeks before Pesaḥ. The rabbi was elated, but the rebbetzin said she would prefer to stay in jail another fourteen days! Whether one follows the letter or the spirit of the law, the preparation for Pesaḥ can be a lot of work. It feels obsessive sometimes. Yet the work produces a set of visual cues that help us connect with the holiday on an emotional as well as a rational level.

The first time Miriam and Amanda hosted a seder, they had to move all the furniture from the living room to the dining room and vice versa in order to have enough table space. When the seder was over, out of inertia they left the two rooms in the special holiday arrangement for the rest of the week. They noticed that the physical act of furniture-moving and the experience of seeing an altered space on a daily basis helped them remember emotionally that something special was going on. They decided to make it their family custom to rearrange the furniture for the week of Pesaḥ.

Cleaning is not usually thought of as a religious experience. In fact, for many couples, cleaning can be a source of great tension. Who does the work? Just how clean does it have to be anyway? What do we keep and what do we throw away? Consider how cleaning in the context of a religiously compelling ritual might shift the energy and allow us as members of a couple to look upon the activity in a new light. Of course, cleaning often involves finding items that need to leave the house altogether, from food that is not eaten during Pesah to clothes that no longer fit, to books for which we have long ago run out of shelves. One of the meaningful parts of the pre-Pesah cleaning ritual can be finding appropriate homes for all the surplus items, from non-Jewish food banks to secondhand charity shops.

At the very end of the often-dreaded cleaning process comes one of the most beautiful moments of the whole Jewish holiday cycle. After the traditional searching for and burning of the leaven, there is a brief acknowledgment that no amount of work can ensure that the job was done 100 percent. So the tradition offers a solution. We say:

> All leaven in my possession, whether I have seen it
> or not, whether I have removed it or not, is hereby
> nullified and ownerless as the dust of the earth.

This is an example of how ritual is truly poetry. Of course the leaven is no less in your possession after saying these words than it was before. But this declaration says, essentially, "We have done everything we can possibly do, and that simply must be enough." The spirit of that statement feels apt for couples as we struggle through the challenges of our lives together. Sometimes we need to work hard on issues, and sometimes we need to say, "It's dust of the earth." Whatever it is, whoever was at fault, we will give it no more of our time or energy.

Asking Questions, Responding to the Questioner

Many seder-goers are enchanted by the spectacle of a small child's asking the traditional Four Questions at the table. On a night when slaves became free, children—who are relatively powerless in relation to adults—are given a starring role. Later, the seder cannot conclude without the children's delivering the *afikoman*. Sometimes there is good-natured haggling as all enjoy this symbolic reversal of power relationships. The Four Questions are a wonderful start to the evening for another reason: They remind us of the value of asking. The youngest child's reciting questions provokes the telling of the story, the very heart of the seder. It is the child's eagerness to notice and to inquire that we choose to celebrate.

How often do we ourselves actually become children again, allowing ourselves to stop and ask a question? When our partners say something to us, we are apt to respond with another statement. Whatever your partner says to you, stop and consider the words. There must be at least one word or idea in the sentence that could be queried. When you ask a question and get an answer, try asking another question. "How was your day?"

"Fine."

"In what way?"

When our partner says something critical, our natural reaction is to counter defensively, or, worse, with an attack. Instead, we can try responding with a curious question, asked with goodwill and a desire to understand. "The way you handle money is wasteful."

"Can you explain how you see me being wasteful?"

On a deeper level, our lives together can become rich with questions. Who are you? What makes you happy? Tell me more.

But asking questions is just the start. Listening to the answers is the other half. True listening is a real challenge. Keeping yourself in a questing mode means always reminding yourself of what you do not know. As partners in a relationship, we should try to know less and ask more.

In addition to encouraging questions, the Haggadah teaches us about how to give answers. The Rabbis noticed that the Torah commands us to tell our children about the Exodus from Egypt not once but four times. The text describes four sons, representing four kinds of children. Since the Rabbis assumed that the Torah wastes no words, they posited that there are four different kinds of children, each needing a different kind of explanation. We are all, at different times in our lives, all four of these children. Therefore, we must always be aware of tailoring our response to the particular person asking a question, recognizing which "child" is present at that moment.

Our partners, too, have many facets. Like the four children in the Haggadah, sometimes they are wise, sometimes rebellious, sometimes simple, and sometimes they do not know how to ask. It might be helpful to realize that a way of being and talking with our partner may work well when he is the "wise child" but not so well on a day (or a year) when he "does not know how to ask." We must constantly be learning and practicing new responses.

Sometimes we become stuck in one of the four modes, per-haps because we were typecast that way at a young age. It might be interesting to spend some time thinking about which child's role each of us most typically played in our growing-up years and how we revert to that child, even at times when it does not serve us well.

If you have a Haggadah, take a look at this section. Fool around with it with your partner. This is a great *hevruta* oppor-tunity. Which kind of children do you think would do best in a marriage to each other? Which kind of child would you like to be married to? Have some fun.

Opening the Door to Hope

As we celebrate our freedom, we not only recall the bitterness of slavery, we put it in our mouths and taste it. While we know that we can eventually mix it with the sweet *haroset,* the first bite must be the horseradish alone in its full power. The Haggadah then tells us that the *haroset* represents the hope that sweetened the bitterness of slavery and helped the Israelites endure it.

There are two very different explanations for the ingredients of *haroset.* One interpretation links it to the bricks that the Israelites were forced to make for Pharaoh; some Jewish communities even maintain the practice of adding a little bit of dirt to the recipe. And, in one famous case, soldiers at war who had no ingredients for the *haroset* simply put a brick on the seder plate.

Others, however, identify *haroset* not with Pharaoh's bricks but with the nuts, fruits, and wine mentioned in the Song of Songs. Since the Song of Songs is traditionally recited at the seder, that makes some sense. So even if you don't want to read one of the great love poems of all times at your seder, you can, quite literally, ingest it.

A legend connects the love poems of the Song of Songs to the story told at the seder. It tells us that, after Pharaoh's decree that all male Israelite babies should be killed, the men's response was to abstain from sex with their wives. But the women were more hopeful. They seduced their husbands in the fields and gave birth under apple trees. Among the children born this way was Moses, who grew up to save his people from slavery. What a beautiful tale of profound hope and courage (along with sex and intimacy)! And how subtle to be able to simply spoon up the sweet stuff and taste it, as it makes the bitter herbs edible, without ever having to mention its secret connection to sexual intimacy.

We may have our own subtle and sweet ways to give each other hope. "Hope is the thing that is left us in a bad time," said E. B. White. Partners must learn how to help each other through the hard times, from the arduous to the trivial. When Marjorie's computer is giving her trouble, her usually pleasant personality vanishes, and she becomes a person possessed. Her husband Leon, who is not at all good with computers, sits with her for hours and tries different strategies to make it work right. One night she said, "There's no point in both of us wasting all this time. You can't fix this any better than I can." But he was not there to fix the computer; he was there to remind her that she was loved. When was the last time you were the harbinger of hope for your partner? What can you do today to help her through some bitterness in her life?

Leaving It Unresolved

The custom of reserving a cup of wine for Elijah the Prophet began because of an argument. There was a debate between the Rabbis concerning the proper number of cups of wine at the seder. Some said four and some said five. The solution was a compromise: The fifth cup would be on the table, but people would not drink from it (*Mishnah Pesaḥ* 10:1).

Why is it called Elijah's Cup? Elijah is the one who is expected to return to earth at the end of time, a time of peace and justice. In the Talmud, when an argument cannot be resolved, the Rabbis often say, "Wait till Elijah the Prophet comes. He will resolve it!" Since the matter of the cups is that kind of dispute, the cup belongs to Elijah.

And it does not hurt, now and again, for us to laugh at our own disputes and conclude that they will be resolved only when Elijah himself returns to earth—probably not anytime soon. Perhaps couples would do well to keep Elijah's Cup in plain view at all times. You might consider designating, buying, or making an Elijah's Cup (or some other object) that you can look to as a reminder that some arguments will not be resolved in our lifetimes. On the other hand, the seder reminds us that our lifetimes are part of a larger story that will end in healing and redemption.

Celebrations/*Minhagim*

Decide on some cleaning that you have been dreading in your home (or perhaps the inside of your car?) and do it together in the spirit of Pesa*h* preparation. Be sure to find worthy recipients for what is edible or usable.

Buy some ritual object or a new Haggadah for the seder.

Bake matzah together. Mix flour, water, and a little bit of salt and oil. Working as quickly as possible, roll it out, punch the holes, and bake it at as high a temperature as possible. No more than eighteen minutes should elapse from the moment the water and flour meet until it is fully cooked. The speed of the work reminds you of the Israelites' haste as they fled Egypt. While the matzah may not be 100 percent kosher for Pesa*h*, it will be edible.

Develop a collection of Haggadot. Pick one Haggadah to be the "family Haggadah" and have all the people you share the seder with sign their names in the book. Over many years this can become a beautiful record of the seders you have celebrated together.

Make *haroset* together, using the Song of Songs to create a recipe. Read the Song of Songs or more contemporary love poetry to each other while preparing the *haroset*. According to Rabbi Isaac Luria, among others, the key is to mix sweet wine and spices with some or all of the fruits and nuts mentioned in the Song of Songs: pomegranates, apples, figs, dates, walnuts, chestnuts, almonds, and raisins.

Learning with a Partner/<u>H</u>evruta

In every generation we are obligated to see ourselves as if we personally went out from Egypt. As it says: You shall tell your child on that very day: It is because of what God did for me when I went out from Egypt.

—**The Passover Haggadah**

Questions for Discussion

If one understands "Egypt" in a political sense as a reign of oppression:

1. What does it mean to you to say that you personally have gone out from Egypt?

2. How would you remember this in your life?

3. What actions would it lead to?

If we understand "Egypt" in a spiritual sense as a "narrow place" in which we are psychologically trapped:

1. What are some of the ways in which you relate to this verse?

2. Have you "gone out from Egypt" in your life?

3. What is the liberation you still hope for?

The Exodus story refers to midwives (likely Egyptians themselves) who, in defiance of Pharaoh's decree, saved the Israelite babies in Egypt (Exodus 1:15–21). Pesa<u>h</u> is a time to ask ourselves questions about righteous behavior in times when it is needed. Watch *Into the Arms of Strangers*, a documentary re-calling how British families saved ten thousand Jewish children from Nazi Germany and Austria in the late 1930s.

Questions for Discussion

1. What are the situations in the world today that we, as a couple, should be addressing as we think about the story of Pesa<u>h</u>?

A good relationship has a pattern like a dance and is built on some of the same rules. The partners do not need to hold on tightly, because they move confidently in the same pattern, intricate but gay and swift and free, like a country dance of Mozart's. To touch heavily would be to arrest the pattern and freeze the movement, to check the endlessly changing beauty of its unfolding. There is no place here for the possessive clutch, the clinging arm, the heavy hand; only the barest touch in passing. Now arm in arm, now face to face, now back to back—it does not matter which. Because they know they are partners moving to the same rhythm, creating a pattern together, and being invisibly nourished by it.

—Anne Morrow Lindbergh

Questions for Discussion

1. What are the rules that form the rhythm to your dance?

2. Are you currently feeling "gay and swift and free"?

3. Are the rules nourishing you?

4. Where do you feel you need to give each other more freedom?

5. Are there new rhythms or rules you want to create for your mutual dance?

Reaching Out/*Gemilut Hesed*

If you are hosting a seder, think about people you know who would really appreciate an invitation. In addition, you can call local colleges or institutions and ask if they have any Jewish students or residents who need a seder to attend. It is also an opportunity to invite foreigners or non-Jews who might not have other opportunities to be part of a seder.

Call your local Jewish Family and Children's Service and see if you can prepare a Pesah meal for a Jew who is homebound. When you deliver the food, make sure you have time to stop and visit.

Look into ways your synagogue could become more hospitable. If it is not already involved, the congregation might want to consider joining a network of religious institutions that help to house homeless people in houses of worship. See the Interfaith Hospitality Network (www.nihn.org).

Make a list of people you would like to host in the coming months and make a schedule together for inviting them into your home.

If you have guest quarters in your home, consider ways to make them more comfortable.

Join the Freecycle listserv in which neighbors post the items they wish to give away and others post items they are seeking. No money changes hands, but new friends are often made. Go to www.freecycle.org and check the area where you live. If your town is not listed, this website will allow you to start such a list for your city or town.

Collect old books for local prisons and jails. Correspond with a prisoner who is believed to be innocent. Information on falsely convicted prisoners is available from Jim McCloskey of Centurion Ministries at www.centurionministries.org.

Shavuot

Shavuot is a late spring harvest holiday. The ancient Israelites called it the Feast of Weeks, _Hag HaShavuot,_ for the seven weeks from the early spring corn harvest to the late spring wheat harvest. According to Leviticus 23:15, we must count off each day and week, from the second seder to Shavuot, taking note of each of the requisite forty-nine days as they pass. This counting (_Sefirat HaOmer_) enables us to determine when Shavuot starts without having to consult a calendar.

The Talmud, compiled well after the Temple was destroyed, when the majority of Jews lived outside Israel, ascribes an entirely new meaning to the festival. It recasts the holiday as a celebration of Israel's receiving the Torah from God at Mount Sinai. The counting of the Omer became a symbolic link between the freedom we gained with our departure from Egypt and the responsibility we took on with our acceptance of the Torah.

The Book of Ruth, with its agricultural backdrop, is read as part of the holiday celebration. Its two major themes—the power of enduring commitment, and the obligation to care for the poor and the stranger—find expression in the holiday's liturgy and customs. Some contemporary liberal Jewish communities celebrate Confirmation on Shavuot, as their teenagers affirm their commitment to live as Jewish adults.

As a symbol of the harvest, many congregations decorate the synagogue with flowers. It is also customary to eat dairy foods on this holiday, symbolizing the belief that the Torah is "milk and honey" to the Jews.

CHAPTER FOUR

Covenantal Loving: Shavuot

*I know how to dream, to listen and to wait. I offer
you my dreams, my silence and my hand.*

—Elie Wiesel (adaptation)

Forty-nine days after the Pesa<u>h</u> seder, amidst graduations,
weddings, and preparations for the arrival of summer, there
is yet another opportunity for celebration in the Jewish annual
cycle—Shavuot. Some associate it with Confirmation services,
flowers adorning the ark, or eating blintzes. In truth, it is a great
time for couples to look at their lives together, for Shavuot is
all about relationships and commitments, about doubts and
reassurances.

For millennia, humanity's farming and herding ancestors
learned repeatedly that no matter how carefully they tended
their land or flocks, some unpredictable act of nature or God
could destroy their work in an instant. Each planting brought renewed expectations, and with them, renewed fears. Through the
growing season and the harvest, these ancient farmers sought re-
assurance that they and the fruits of their labor would survive.

The Torah states: "You shall observe the Feast of Weeks [Shavuot], of the first fruits of the wheat harvest" (Exodus 34:22); "And on the day of the first fruits, your Feast of Weeks, when you bring an offering of new grain to Adonai, you shall observe a sacred occasion" (Numbers 28:26); "You shall count off seven weeks; start to count the seven weeks when the sickle is first put to the standing grain. Then you shall observe the Feast of Weeks for Adonai your God, offering your freewill contribution according as Adonai your God has blessed you" (Deuteronomy 16:9–10).

Many cultures developed rites of thanksgiving after the harvest, when they were surrounded by the earth's abundance. Understanding their bounty as a gift, they expressed their gratitude to a multitude of sources, acknowledging that they were dependent on forces beyond themselves with which they had ongoing relationships. The ancient Israelites offered their thanks for their harvests to the one God of Israel, responsible for all of creation.

Later generations found meaning in the original holiday's emphasis on relationship with a power beyond themselves, but they no longer restricted themselves to agricultural proofs for God's existence. Instead, they affirmed their relationship to God through a new metaphor, derived from the Torah. Unlike their ancestors, whose dependence on nature inextricably bound them to a deity, the Rabbis taught that the people of Israel had freely and willingly bound themselves to God through a covenant. This new relationship, based on mutual commitments between God and the people of Israel in the form of the commandments offered and accepted at Sinai (Exodus 20), created a deep and enduring existential and spiritual bond, with its own unique demands and rewards. Shavuot became linked with Sinai; the gift of Torah and the gift of the harvest were both signs of the Israelites' eternal relationship with God.

Despite this radically new interpretation, there was no need to change the festival's name. Shavuot has two meanings in Hebrew: "weeks," and "oaths" or "pledges." We could continue to count the weeks between the Pesah harvest and the first fruits of late spring and we could remember and affirm the pledges made at Sinai, both at the same time!

Covenantal Loving

The ancient Israelite prophets referred to the enduring relationship between God and Israel as a marriage. Extending this metaphor further, the medieval mystics suggested in the *Zohar*, a classic text of Jewish mysticism, that Shavuot was the wedding day of God and Israel. For the prophets and the mystics alike, the Torah's description of Israel's relationship with God, based on a covenant, mirrored the human marriages they knew. Both began with a glorious day of pledges, followed by years of living in the real world with its strains, challenges, hardships, and vagaries, as well as its joys, pleasures, satisfactions, and delights. In the Bible stories, they saw God and Israel arguing and caressing, disappointing and reconciling, all the while trying to maintain the love that led them to make a covenant with each other in the first place.

Today at our weddings we pledge our love and speak of our shared hopes and dreams that our commitments will endure. We usually accentuate our similarities and minimize our differences. We bind our existence to each other, materially, spiritually, and emotionally. Shavuot can be a time for us to celebrate our relationships anew, reflecting on the ways they have evolved over time. Alternatively, our anniversaries can represent our personal Shavuots. Like our ancestors we can recall what we had intended to plant and consider whether or not we have succeeded in producing the harvest we sought.

At many Jewish weddings, couples sign a written document known as a *ketubah*, a Jewish wedding contract. While the *ketubah* has had a long history as a legal financial contract, the modern liberal *ketubah* articulates the shared values that the couple hope to nurture during their life together. On Shavuot couples can look back at their original pledges, commitments, and expectations, whether they were expressed in their original vows, in letters, or in a *ketubah*, to see how they have changed over time. We can share the specific moments and explicit ways we have felt most secure in our love, as well as the occasions when we were filled with doubts about the strength of our bond. With or without a *ketubah*, we can set aside time to reflect together upon whether or not the give-and-take of our relationship is meeting our needs.

Covenantal loving requires continued openness: openness toward our partners as they change and evolve, to new opportunities as they present themselves, to new perspectives in our relationship. The covenant at Sinai was made in the desert, on a mountaintop. The Rabbis saw the desert as the quintessential open space, and they taught that we must be open like the desert, in order to receive wisdom, instruction, and new insights—precisely what God offered Israel at Sinai. Ideally, this is what we offered our partners at our weddings, and what we continue to offer each other today.

The Kabbalists of the sixteenth century developed a custom of staying up throughout the night on Shavuot in order to study. They called this study session "making repairs (*tikkun*) on the eve (*leil*) of Shavuot." They understood their practice as keeping an all-night vigil before the "wedding" the next morning between God and Israel. The intensity of the late-night hours and the exhaustion due to lack of sleep were meant to create a greater sense of openness, through the vast timelessness of the night, the better to prepare for the messages of Sinai and the renewal of the covenant. The mystics who introduced this custom had a holistic view of the cosmos. They taught that everything done on earth had reverberations and consequences for the world, for the universe, and for the heavens. They believed spending the eve of Shavuot in this way could improve the life of the individual and the world. For, in this heightened and limitless state, we can hear new meanings, sense new possibilities, and consider new commitments that can have a reparative effect on our lives.

As a couple, you surely know the constraints that come from day-to-day routine. Just keeping on schedule and accomplishing what you set out to do in the course of a day, a week, a month, often preclude your really experiencing open time. We can benefit from taking advantage of undemarcated time by incorporating the essence of *Tikkun Leil Shavuot* into our lives. In advance, we can identify our next "busy season" and schedule time to enjoy the slower pace that follows. Can the two of you take time, even just one night, to heighten your senses, focus your attention on each other, and open yourselves to an enriching, reparative experience together?

Contracts and Covenants

In our long-term loving relationships we have both implicit and explicit rules—contracts—that govern our daily interactions. These contracts comprise the overarching covenant that we commit to willingly for our existential, spiritual, and emotional growth and well-being. We have contracts about meals and family interactions and sex and fighting and reconciling. We have contracts about language and displays of affection and holiday observances. We have contracts about work and play. As in the stories in the Bible that take place after the making of the covenant at Sinai, when God and Israel measured the power of their commitment with explicit actions, we see our actions toward each other as signs of our love and commitment, our adherence to our covenant.

Some of us might wish for a long, detailed rulebook with explanatory notes clarifying all the ambiguities in our relationships—something like a "relationship Torah"! Unfortunately, there is no such thing. Mostly we share generalities with each other. "Yes, we agreed we would have kids. But how many? And when?" "Yes, we agreed we would have a Jewish home. But does that mean no Christmas tree?" But sometimes our agreements are too specific. "Yes, we agreed we would celebrate Thanksgiving with your parents at their home. But that was when we lived on the same coast!" "Yes, we agreed I would do most of the housework, but that was when I worked part-time and was home with the children."

Neither we nor our relationships are static. The curious thing about the contracts we have is that we often become aware of them only in the breach, when we find ourselves confused or hurt: "We never said you had to call home if you were staying at work late, but you always did. Tonight, when I hadn't heard from you by 8:30 and I called because I was worried, you got upset that I interrupted you! I was hurt and angry." At some point it becomes necessary for us to make explicit our expectations and to clarify a mutually acceptable compromise. We rework our contracts, guided by the hope of maintaining our covenant.

From the time Peter and Arlene were in college, they were in the habit of taking and paying back loans, holding down multiple jobs, and scrimping and saving. The day Arlene got a huge raise, she went out and bought a luxury they had long denied themselves—a Caribbean vacation just for the two of them. Rather than rejoicing, Peter got angry. He went on the vacation reluctantly, unable to relax and enjoy himself. He had trouble adjusting to their change in fortune. In all the years they'd been together, they'd never discussed how they would alter their lives if their incomes were to exceed their needs—in their early years this possibility was no more than a pipe dream. Now that it had become a reality, they needed to renegotiate their implicit contract about finances.

Carl's father died when he was eight. Carl had told his partner, Fred, about his father's illness and had made brief mention of his having found his father dead one afternoon when he came home from school. Since Carl hadn't elaborated on it, Fred hadn't pressed. He figured he would learn more about what that moment had been like for Carl in due time. However, "due time" never came. Fred sensed that Carl had strong feelings and wanted to let him know that it was OK to talk about them, but recognized that over time they had created an implicit "contract" not to broach the subject. One day, after a lovely afternoon together, Fred decided to risk breaking it, and asked Carl very directly to share with him the events of that life-altering afternoon. Carl was relieved that Fred had taken the lead in opening this new level of communication between them.

When Roberta stopped eating meat, Jon was more than a bit surprised. He hadn't thought twice about her references to vegetarianism in the past. She was a voracious reader, and this seemed to be just another interesting modern ethical idea she had come across. The first week or two after Roberta gave up red meat Jon was really supportive and ate all the vegetarian dishes she prepared. But he began seriously to crave red meat. Adopting vegetarianism represented far more than Roberta's personal choice. It had a major impact on both of them and their life together. They were going to have to figure out how best to adapt to their current needs, desires, and expectations.

In order for a committed loving relationship to last, both partners must learn the profound lesson that the relationship is an entity itself and *its* needs must be considered equally with those of each member. By making a commitment, we are choosing not to function any longer as a completely independent being. It's not that we cease to be individuals; we will remain two distinct individuals with different personalities, needs, strengths, and beliefs. Any change in one will affect the other. More significantly, however, it will also have an impact on the relationship as a whole. Sometimes the effect will be minor and will be easily incorporated into our lives. At other times, we will have to make an effort to discuss and work out a new agreement with our partner. When we succeed in doing this well, our covenant grows stronger.

Jewish history is an ongoing story of a people trying to understand a covenant: Specific rules often need reinterpretation; generalities need to be made more specific. Even the laws enumerated in that covenant, though seemingly concise and clear—such as the prescription of death for one who breaks the Sabbath (Exodus 31:14–15)—must be reinterpreted in light of changed circumstances and perceptions. And as for the broad statements of that mythic covenant, each generation of Jews has to translate into meaningful contemporary actions laws such as "Love your neighbor as yourself" (Leviticus 19:18) or "Be holy as God is holy" (Leviticus 19:2). The covenants on which we build our relationships can be equally challenging to live out.

While many people assume that there is only one definition of fidelity, each individual and each couple has its own understanding of this concept. Each relationship could benefit from regular discussions of expectations in this area, yet few couples actually have them. But our relationships will be strengthened if we acknowledge that one person's ideas about what constitutes fidelity can be different from the other's, and may change over time. Like the Jewish tradition's ongoing process of reexamining a covenant in light of changing circumstances, our committed long-term relationships benefit from a similar process.

When Marla and Tony first were dating, he thought it was cute that she flirted with all the men in the restaurant, including the waiter. Now he experiences it as annoying—a sign of her blatant disregard for the depth of their commitment.

In college, Wendy's best friend had been a man, but it was never an issue between her and her partner, Aaron. Now she has grown close with a coworker, Todd, and when one night she decided to have dinner with him, Aaron was furious and accused her of being unfaithful.

For years, Greg and Tom had agreed that sleeping with a stranger while away on business was not a breach of their covenant, whereas an ongoing affair would be. Now that Tom was in a long-term care facility due to advanced multiple sclerosis and was physically unable to respond to Greg, they both agreed that Greg deserved to have an ongoing physical relationship with someone else, without its being a violation of their commitment to each other.

Annette was stunned when her best friend, Donna, didn't share her joy at having found someone to love just months after Doug, Annette's husband of thirty-five years, had died. Annette and Doug had spoken before his death, and he had said he hoped she would be able to love again and find someone else to grow old with. Donna didn't hear any of this. From her perspective, it was too fast, too soon; Annette was being unfaithful to Doug's memory.

There's no way to know what your partner thinks about fidelity unless you discuss it. There's no way to understand your partner's perceptions and perspectives, or to have your partner understand yours, unless you share your beliefs and concerns and worries, as well as your reactions to the ways people you know have dealt with this issue. Only through open dialogue—even if prompted by a breach—will you be able to gain greater clarity about your covenant in this area.

Affairs do not invariably lead to divorce. In fact, many couples find that in the wake of an affair they can renegotiate their covenant, their commitment to be married, if they recognize the need to incorporate both some parts of their old contract and some new guidelines based on their revised expectations and promises.

Think of the covenant you made with your partner as a precious glass. A glass is both strong and fragile. It can hold an infinite number of different liquids, as long as its integrity isn't compromised. But when we handle a glass we must remember that it is also fragile, and if we don't treat it with care and gentleness we run the risk of breaking it. We must try our best to constantly tend to our covenant. If its integrity seems threatened, we need to check whether it is still intact enough for us to continue using it, and repair it if not. We need to be mindful of what we put into it and how we handle it, so that we can continue to draw sustenance and joy from it.

Loving-kindness: Above and beyond the Rules

Covenantal loving involves much more than contractual responsibilities. On Shavuot we remind ourselves how important it is that we move beyond the established rules and engage with our partners more fully and intimately. Shavuot provides us with a model for this extraordinary type of love with the annual reading of the Book of Ruth. A Moabite by birth, Ruth marries an Israelite man who is living in Moab with his family. When the man, his father, and his brother die, his mother, Naomi, urges her daughter-in-law Ruth to remain in Moab with her own kin. But Ruth feels bound to Naomi; she feels a connection that extends beyond the contract that made them in-laws. She chooses to remain with the widow Naomi and return with her to Israel to care for her. They arrive in Israel homeless and poor. Ruth is able to feed the two of them by gleaning from the fields belonging to Naomi's extended family.

We too have the ability to offer our partners voluntary or unexpected signs of our love and commitment. We can show our love when we put into words the joy and sense of caring that our partner kindles in us, when we show up unexpectedly at a doctor's office because our partner expressed anxiety about the appointment, or when we know our partner is too busy to phone an ailing cousin so we do it instead. We can show our love when we bring home flowers on a particularly dismal day, or when we put a hand out and gently touch our beloved to soothe away tensions. Such small kindnesses go far beyond the formal pledges we've made and reinforce our intimate bonds with each other.

The biblical law that supported the widowed Naomi and Ruth states: "When you reap the harvest of your land, you shall not reap all the way to the edges of your field, or gather the gleanings of your harvest. You shall not pick your vineyard bare, or gather the fallen fruit of your vineyard; you shall leave them for the poor and the stranger: I, Adonai, am your God" (Leviticus 19:9–10). This has become a major influence on Jewish ethical behavior, and serves as the basis for our obligations to care for the stranger and those less fortunate than ourselves to this day.

There are specific aspects of our day-to-day exchanges with our partners that reassure us that we are truly loved. It is important to let each other know when these moments occur. That way, you or your partner can consciously choose to repeat the behavior in the future. From the time Diana was a child, she was soothed by a gentle hand stroking her hair. Her adult partner, Jack, occasionally did this as part of his attempts to calm her when she was upset. One night Diana told Jack how powerful this particular form of comfort was for her when she was feeling most vulnerable. From then on, he was always able to reassure her, with this simple but meaningful gesture, that he was there to love and support her.

And with our partner we can demonstrate our love and care for our children or other members of younger generations. We can leave them with vibrant models from which to draw in the future when we consciously make efforts to put into practice the values we most cherish. We can also follow a custom begun by Jews in the Middle Ages of preparing ethical wills. In addition to whatever legal papers they drew up, stipulating the dispersion of material goods, our ancestors recognized that a significant part of their legacy was found in the values and teachings that they had lived by, aspired to, and taught to others.

You can set aside some time together to see what values you have tried to live by, what values you have tried to impart, and find a way to put them in writing so that those you love can re-member you by them in the future. You can write an ethical will during Shavuot or at some other time that works for the two of you. Over the years, you can revisit and refine your ethical wills, reflecting on the changes you make as you grow.

Counting Time/Making Time Count

Covenantal loving depends both on promises and on time, the two central concepts of the word *Shavuot*. Only with time can we see if our pledges and expectations evolve and find full ex-pression. According to Jewish tradition, to reach the festival of Shavuot we count from one established marker to another. In our daily lives, too, we often utilize this form of counting when we are anticipating something special: five days until vacation, two months until my promotion.

But this is only one of the ways we count and mark time. Following a major life event, we often count time as if it began with that event: three years cancer-free, four months since we got married, ten months since my mother died. Imagine what it would be like for us to utilize this form of counting within our relationships to heighten our sensitivity to particularly important moments.

Joel and Shoshana started counting from the first night that Joel retired. Joel had longed for the day he could leave the agency where he'd worked for over thirty years. His departure was truly a new beginning for them both. He was more relaxed than he had been in years. The Joel who had regularly surfaced during vacations and on occasional weekends was now present most of the time. Retirement became a way for him to reengage the world outside the office. He began to volunteer as a mentor, sharing his life experience and professional expertise with others. He had time to read for pleasure and to do chores around the house. The changes in him reduced Shoshana's stress level as well. They both gratefully counted the days since this new stage of life began for them.

If we count each day, we are less likely to find that time has slipped away without our noticing. How often have we found ourselves commenting: "Wow ... it's already July? It seems like spring just started!" We don't remember the specifics of our lives. We don't account for our time. Counting our days is an invitation to make our days count. To be aware of each day's passage challenges us to consider what we did with our time, and whether we used our time in the best possible ways for us.

Celebrations/*Minhagim*

If you have a *ketubah*:

- Review it with each other and discuss possible changes to it.

- Consider having it framed or reframed and displaying it in a special place in your home.

If you don't have a *ketubah*, consider making one:

- Discuss what you would like it to say.

- If you are so inclined, have a calligrapher make a work of art from your words.

Choose three dates in the not-too-distant future; decide now that you will take time—the evening, the morning, the afternoon, the whole day—to be together, without a specific plan to *do* anything.

Do something you know your partner would love, that you have never before taken the time to do.

Consider preparing ethical wills as a way of gaining clarity for yourselves about what you most value at this stage of your life:

- Share them with each other.

- Let those who might eventually receive them know of their existence.

- Save them in a safe place.

Learning with a Partner/<u>H</u>evruta

Entreat me not to leave you, or to return from following after you. For wherever you go, I will go; and

*where you lodge, I will lodge; your people shall be
my people, and your God my God. Where you die, I
will die, and there will I be buried.*

—**Ruth 1:16–17**

Questions for Discussion

1. How do these promises resonate with you?

2. Do you anticipate that you will always live in the same place, share the same religion, be buried in the same place?

3. What promises were you ready to make at the beginning of your relationship?

4. What promises are you willing to make today? If there are changes, do you understand what precipitated them?

*Give me your tired, your poor,
Your huddled masses yearning to breathe free,
The wretched refuse of your teeming shore.
Send these, the homeless, tempest-tost to me,
I lift my lamp beside the golden door!*

—**Emma Lazarus**

Questions for Discussion

1. Who are the poor, the huddled masses, the homeless, in your midst?

2. Who do you perceive as strangers?

3. How do you treat them?

4. What else could you be doing to enhance their lives?

*A love that depends on one thing lasts only as long
as that thing.
Love that does not depend on a particular thing
never dies away.*

—*Pirkei Avot* 5:16

Questions for Discussion

1. What are some of the things you first loved about your partner that have not endured?

2. What intangible things help your love endure?

3. What are some of the things you still love about your partner, that keep your love alive?

4. On what does your love depend that is enduring?

Reaching Out/*Gemilut Hesed*

Take either the literal or figurative corners of your field, in whatever type of work you engage, and make it available to someone other than yourself.

- Volunteer as a mentor.

- Distribute your pocket change to needy individuals or set it aside for a charitable gift.

Work with a political action group dedicated to the rights of new immigrants.

Volunteer to do diversity training at a local school.

Register new voters.

If you and your partner enjoy gardening, plant flowers where they will be appreciated—a nursing home, an urban park.

- If making flowers grow is not an interest of yours, send flowers to someone who needs some beauty in her life.

Rosh Hashanah

Rosh Hashanah, which literally means "head of the year," is the Jewish New Year. Rosh Hashanah marks the beginning of a ten-day period of repentance, ending with Yom Kippur. The concept of *teshuvah*, repenting and returning, is at the heart of this festival season. The month preceding Rosh Hashanah, known as Elul, is also a period of self-reflection and introspection. Rosh Hashanah and Yom Kippur are known as the *Yamim Noraim*, the Days of Awe, also called the High Holy Days.

Rosh Hashanah itself is a joyous fall holiday. Many Jews celebrate by gathering for festive meals and attending synagogue services, where they hear the New Year announced with the blowing of the shofar, a ram's horn. The use of a shofar dates back to biblical times: "Blast piercing notes upon the shofar for the New Moon, for the full moon, for our festive holiday" (Psalm 81:4–5).

We eat special foods to enhance our celebration of the New Year. To underscore the cycle of life, we eat round foods such as apples and ḥallah, an egg-bread also eaten on Shabbat and other holidays; on Rosh Hashanah it is round, whereas at other times it is oblong and braided. As a symbol of our hope for a sweet New Year, we dip the apples in honey, and eat special cakes and cookies made with honey.

CHAPTER FIVE

Connecting with Community and with Each Other: Rosh Hashanah

*I have perceiv'd that to be with those I like is
    enough,
To stop in company with the rest at evening is
    enough,
To be surrounded by beautiful, curious, breathing,
    laughing flesh is enough,
To pass among them or touch any one, or rest my
    arm ever so lightly round his or her neck for a
    moment, what is this then?
I do not ask any more delight, I swim in it as in a
    sea.
There is something in staying close to men and
    women and looking on them, and in the contact
    and odor of them, that pleases the soul well,
All things please the soul, but these please the soul
    well.*

—Walt Whitman

The summer is over and everything feels different. The air is moving, people are moving, school buses are rolling, and daylight is shorter. Our daily pace picks up, and we begin again our "normal" routines. The sights and sounds of the neighborhood are returning to a more familiar and predictable rhythm, and the office or school or hospital or shop is resuming its usual hum and bustle. How easy it is to mindlessly return to what is known, to reengage without reviewing or assessing who we are and how we and our world have changed or where we want to go in the future. However, the confluence of Rosh Hashanah and these fall events challenges us to look at what we have taken for granted and to consider the possibility of perceiving and organizing ourselves and our worlds in new and different ways.

"Days are like scrolls; write on them what you want to be remembered," said Rabbi Ba<u>h</u>ya Ibn Pekuda. We all remember the fresh, clean notebooks we bought as students each September, the empty pages waiting to be filled. So the days of our new year wait for us to fill them. At this season, we can choose to parallel the transitions abounding in the natural world and our social worlds with tangible personal changes.

Connecting with Community

Join a community, by which alone your work can be made universal and eternal in its results.

—Samson Raphael Hirsch

For many, Rosh Hashanah marks the first time they reconnect with synagogue and community after a summer away. For others, it is one of a few times in the year they explicitly gather with other Jews. Rosh Hashanah often serves as a way for people to (re)connect with communities larger than themselves, sometimes just for the day, sometimes for much longer. Our relationships with our spouses unfold in the context of the outside world, to which we each connect in our own unique ways. Our challenge as a couple is to honor our *individual* relationships with the larger world at the same time that we build connections with that world together.

Jewish writings over the millennia have stressed the importance of being part of a community, of sharing our lives with others. It is within community, not just with our families, that we welcome our newest members at circumcisions and baby-namings. At weddings, it is with our community that we welcome a newly created family into our midst. And at death, it is with the help of our community that we bury our dead and mourn them. In fact, Jewish tradition states that certain prayers can be offered only when we are in a community of at least ten, a minyan. While home may be a beloved and cherished oasis, there are times we must move beyond its borders and join with larger groups.

For some of us this comes naturally, easily. We actively seek out others with whom we can share all aspects of our lives. We may even have found a particular group to call our own. Many people belong to one or more groups very comfortably for years. Yet there are times when we realize that we have continued to belong to a group even after it has ceased meeting our needs or expectations. Finally, some of us find groups demanding or oppressive, a source of anxiety rather than comfort. And this only describes us as individuals!

Discovering groups that are comfortable for both members of a couple can be an enormous challenge. When it comes to finding communities of meaning, spiritual and religious communities that can meet our individual needs along with our needs as a couple, it can become truly daunting. Just choosing where to go for Rosh Hashanah (a synagogue—large or small, traditional

Our relationship with and responsibility for the world are encapsulated in a rabbinic story, or midrash: "Before creating the world, God made world after world and discarded each of them, saying: 'This does not please me.' At last God created this one and said: 'This one is good!' God then made Adam and showed him all the world. God said: 'Look at this beautiful world! Take good care of it; do not abuse or destroy it, for I am done with making worlds. If you ruin this one, there will be none to follow it.'"

or liberal—or a gathering of friends or family—whose?) can make even two Jews feel thoroughly overwhelmed.

Some of us once found an acceptable compromise—"for the kids' sake." Then we were left wondering what to do when the kids grew up, or what to do when we were confronted with each others' differing personal predilections. Consider which communities you would choose to join today, and why. Take a look at the communities you currently belong to and ask yourselves what they offer you now, what you offer them, and what together you offer the world. With the limited time you have, should you join only groups that affirm your most cherished values? And, if your long-established communities no longer work for you, should you work to change the community or seek out a new one?

When Eve and Marnie first joined the synagogue chorus, they were eager to meet people in their neighborhood. For a number of years their social life revolved around the chorus, and they were delighted that it was a part of their lives. Five years later, when for the umpteenth time they found they were dragging themselves, grumbling, to a rehearsal, Marnie asked the question they'd been avoiding: "Why are we doing this?" It took them a few more weeks to review what the chorus had meant to them. They grew to understand that their original reasons for joining had long ago ceased to exist, and the social demands they felt from the other chorus members had become a burden. With sincere thanks for some wonderful years, they bid the chorus good-bye and joined a new chorus, where singing together, but not socializing afterwards, was the only expectation.

Our Place in the Larger World

The communities we belong to are as small as a book club or coop shift, and as broad as the universe. On Rosh Hashanah we recognize that we are one part of a much larger natural world, and we stand with all of creation to celebrate its existence and contemplate our part in its survival.

The world as we know it is in some ways strikingly similar to the world described in the Bible:

> *Praise God from the earth:*
> *Crocodiles, creatures of the deep,*
> *Fire and hail, snow and mist,*
> *Storm winds that obey the divine command;*
> *Mountains and hills,*
> *Fruit trees and cedars,*
> *Animals and cattle,*
> *Creatures that creep and birds on the wing.*
>
> —*Psalm 148:1–10*

The sky and the seas, the mountains, plants, and animals continue to exist and evoke in us the same sense of awe, majesty, and wonder that the psalmists expressed thousands of years ago.

Yet in some ways, our world is markedly different. Species have become extinct. The fox and bear and coyote populations have been displaced by housing developments. Rivers have dried up, their riverbeds becoming arid and cracked. Acid rain, deforestation, and global warming threaten the very survival of the

Classic Jewish texts identify Rosh Hashanah as
the "birthday of the
world." "Rabbi Eliezer
said: 'In Tishrei the world
was created'" (*Rosh
Hashanah* 27a). "Rabbi
Yehoshua differs with
Rabbi Eliezer, stating that
the world was created in
Nissan but these and
these are the words of
the living God. And we
should assume that in
Tishrei, the thought to
create came up in [God's]
mind, but it was not
brought into creation until
Nissan" (Tosafot to *Rosh
Hashanah* 27a).

world as we and all our ancestors have known it. As we celebrate the birthday of the world, we have a choice: to contribute to its further destruction or to commit ourselves to maintaining and caring for it.

Will we recognize and accept our place in the created world and act responsibly toward this largest of communities?

Ted and Merle had been members of the Ocean Conservancy for many years. They believed in the goals of the organization and enjoyed the time they spent with other members of the group. One winter they joined with a group of Conservancy members on a trip to Maui. They and their companions watched with joy as the whales and dolphins leaped around in the pristine water. This vacation reinforced for them their enduring commitment to preserving the natural world.

Individually and together, the two of you can pledge yourselves to affirming your place in creation. You can find local and global means to repair the ills that our society has wrought and to bring to the world a more habitable and hospitable environment. You can enrich your relationship whether you participate in these activities together or apart. When engaging in acts of *tikkun olam* together, you can have the joy of sharing an experience and discussing it afterwards, learning how each of you perceived the interactions and felt about what you were doing. Individually, you can have the joy of engaging with like-minded others and then sharing your experience and perceptions with your partner afterwards.

Connecting with Each Other

As Rosh Hashanah calls us to deepen our commitment to the broader world, it also calls us to enrich our relationships with those we love. The world we inhabit as partners is one that, together, we form, shape, and breathe life into.

We create the "soul" of our relationship; we are the only ones who can assess whether it is enhancing our lives or taking our life's breath from us. Rosh Hashanah offers us the chance to examine this soul, to see if it is evolving as we want it to, to see if we are caring for it and demonstrating our love and commitment to it in all the ways that we can. It reminds us that we are engaged in an ongoing, life-sustaining project with our partners, for which we are accountable and for which we can express our mutual gratitude, not just annually, but daily.

Mindy looked at Tim across the dinner table. The table was small, but the distance between

As part of the traditional morning liturgy, we recite a prayer called *Elohai Neshamah*, which goes like this: "The soul that You have given me, O God, is pure. You have created it. You have formed it. You have breathed it into me, and within me you sustain it. So long as I have breath, therefore, I will give thanks to You, Adonai my God and God of all ages, Guide of all deeds, Sovereign of all souls. Blessed are You, Eternal One, in whose hands are the souls of all the living and the spirits of all flesh."

them seemed enormous. She had been working crazy hours at the office and neither of them could remember a night in the recent past when she hadn't come home completely exhausted. She didn't see any end in sight for her work woes, but she couldn't tolerate the thought of feeling so removed from Tim. She reached out and put her hand on his. When he looked up, she said, "I've missed you." Her eyes filled with tears. He nodded in agreement. They put their forks down and talked about the void they'd each been feeling and their mutual fears that the breach that had developed would be beyond repair.

When we realize that something in our relationship is taking our life's breath rather than replenishing it, when we fear that our relationship is losing its soul, we can engage in an act of *tikkun*. We can challenge ourselves and each other to reject the status quo, turning toward each other to seek new options together. We can reaffirm our desire to form, shape, and breathe life into our relationship.

At Rosh Hashanah we do *teshuvah*, turning both outward and inward to examine our lives. We attempt to return to our essence and to turn away from behaviors and attitudes that diminish us. We review the past year, repent for what we've done wrong, and imagine how we can live better in the coming year. Traditionally at this time we are told to turn to God, often referred to as our Beloved. It may be that exploring new ways to turn to God becomes a meaningful personal spiritual exercise for one or both of you. In addition, as members of a couple, you may find that exploring new ways to turn toward your earthly beloved, returning to each other, can enrich your relationship in profound ways.

Making Changes

Change, even when we perceive it as a positive, even when it is inevitable, is never easy. Human beings seem to be hardwired to resist change. Intuitively we seem to understand the truth of

Anatole France's words, "All changes, even the most longed for, have their melancholy; for what we leave behind is a part of ourselves; we must die to one life before we can enter into another." For some people transitions are so fraught with anxiety that they spend large amounts of their waking energy anticipating and trying to control every last detail, in an attempt to micromanage change. Others, equally anxious, do everything within their power to ignore transitions altogether, choosing instead to deal with them "in the moment," often finding themselves rushed and unprepared when "the moment" finally arrives.

Jewish tradition developed a unique approach for confronting change that can be a model for transition throughout our lives. The departure of an old year and the arrival of a new one are givens. Rather than ignoring them, Jewish customs are designed to prepare us for the change. There is a tradition of sounding the shofar each morning during the month of Elul. Like an alarm clock, it focuses our attention on the inevitable. Its blast tells us that change is in the offing. Will you? Have you? How might you?

By pausing briefly each day to refocus our attention and energy, we can prepare ourselves for change. If the sound of a shofar blast doesn't work for you, try introducing something into your routine for the month leading up to Rosh Hashanah that will serve the same function. Set a PDA alarm to go off during your commute or leave a message as a screensaver to remind you to pause, reflect, and prepare. Perhaps you can use a similar technique whenever you are aware of a major change to come.

We are not expected to take a month off from the tasks of daily living in order to contemplate change. Rather, the tradition teaches that it is precisely through ongoing relationships with others and through continued engagement with the broader world that we gain clarity about whether or not we are living the lives we wish, or want, or need to live.

Laurie and Kate have an annual Elul custom. They go for a long walk and talk about how they have experienced the last year—its highs and lows, its challenges, and its moments of joy and gratitude. They talk about the growth they have each experienced, the regrets they've had. They each speak about themselves. They offer memories and insights about each other. They talk about the character traits that they admire in each other and the times that these were most clearly evident. They discuss the improvements each had hoped to make but were unable to achieve fully. And they muse aloud with each other about the ways they can help and encourage each other to grow in the future. They review the past year of their relationship, often discovering that moments that seemed less than noteworthy for one have left a lasting impression on the other. They talk about how they would like to shape their time together in the coming year to better meet their individual and combined hopes and needs.

This sounds harder than it actually is. Once you start, the discussion takes on a life of its own. The key is to focus on yourself, without criticizing your partner. Perhaps this kind of intimate review is appealing to you but early fall is not the best time to try it. You may find that an anniversary, a birthday, the beginning or end of vacation is your Elul, the time you both feel is ideal for you to engage in what the Rabbis called *heshbon hanefesh*, a soul-reckoning. The act of *teshuvah* is what's important, not the time of year you choose to do it.

Being There

We can turn toward each other with greater focus and care on a daily basis as well. There is a Hebrew phrase that conveys the intensity of this turning toward each other: "*Hineini*—Here I am. Behold me." It appears in both the prayers and the Torah reading for Rosh Hashanah. Traditionally, the cantor turns to God and chants a prayer called *Hineini*, which expresses the hope that God will hear the sincerity of the prayers being offered. And in the Torah story when Isaac calls to his father, unsure about the meaning of their trek up the mountain, Abraham reassures him by saying, "*Hineini*" (Genesis 22:6–8). In each place, the phrase expresses two essential messages. The first is: "I am here; I, myself; I am bringing my whole self to you; I am as present as I can be." The second meaning is: "Behold me; take a look at me; see me for who I am."

Max loved to fix things—a broken leg on a chair, a problem at work. If presented with a problem, he'd jump in ready to find a solution. So whenever Pam was upset, he'd switch into his "fix it" mode. He'd ask questions, believing that if only he had all the facts, he'd be able to make things better. But the more questions he asked, the more upset Pam would become. Time and again, precisely when Max wanted to be there for Pam, he felt ineffectual and rejected. But when he would get up to leave, Pam would become even more upset, saying, "I need you; I want you to be with me! Don't you know that when I'm upset, I don't like to be alone?" She just wanted to be supported but didn't know how to explain this. And so it went, time and time again: Max feeling helpless and rebuffed; Pam feeling badgered, not understood. One day Max happened to put his hand on her thigh and stroke it as she talked. When he asked his next question, Pam lifted up her finger: "Shh, this is what I need, not questions. Having you here with me, loving me, touching me, makes me feel better." Max was still frustrated that he couldn't "fix it," but he finally understood that he was doing something of value by just being there in a loving way with Pam.

Hineini represents the essence of true relationship. It expresses both urgency and risk. The process of *teshuvah* challenges us to consider how honest and open we are being with ourselves and with each other. We need to work on being truly present when our partners turn to us. It isn't always easy. But we can explore together new and more effective ways of saying *Hineini* to each other.

Sometimes looking at the predictable cycles of our lives can help us be more present for each other. There are cycles that are visible to family and friends: career highs and lows; engagement in political or other causes dear to your heart; times of focusing on extended family; times focused on yourselves. There are also cycles that are only known to the two of you: the anxiety produced by the expectation of an annual family gathering; the sadness that accompanies the anniversary of a parent's death; the pressure engendered by the semiannual evaluation at work. Being aware of your partner's cycles may help you offer the kind of support that will be most helpful.

During the weeks before and during the first two long-range planning retreats Zack's company held, he became emotionally unavailable and unresponsive at home, leaving Barbara feeling rejected and ignored. Because they hadn't ever talked about this, she tried to intervene and take care of him in some way. Once they did speak, she understood that it was better for her and Zack if she lowered her expectations of him, and went to visit friends or family or took on a short-term project during that time. That way, both her caretaking and caregiving needs would be satisfied. Barbara learned to work around Zack's needs for these intervals. Zack in turn learned to appreciate Barbara's "self-sacrifice" and to show her extra attention afterwards.

Take some time together to reflect on the predictable cycles of your year. Identify the times when each of you tends to feel most energized, most preoccupied, most at ease. Consider how you can use the highs and lows of your professional or volunteer lives to your best advantage, to enhance your lives the most. Think of how you can turn your time of introspection together into something sweet and hopeful for both of you, just as we dip the <u>h</u>allah into honey at Rosh Hashanah. Find ways to rejoice in the fruits of your labor and savor the richness they bring to your lives. These are issues to think about and discuss honestly together, quite specifically. In this way, you will nourish your relationship's soul, expanding the intimacy and integrity that you've already created with each other.

Celebrations/Minhagim

Before you write a check to renew membership in your synagogue or other communities, take time to share with each other:

- A recollection of a community that was very important to you.

- A time in your life you were nurtured by a community.

Make a New Year's resolution to do one thing to enhance a community to which you already belong or to find a new community reflective of your current interests or needs.

Commit to having something serve as your shofar during the weeks before Rosh Hashanah, to alert you to pause, even briefly, in recognition that the year is coming to an end.

- One day during that pause, discuss with your partner the ways you normally approach transitions.

- How would you change things this year to enhance the time you have together?

- What do you see as your strengths and weaknesses in this area?

- How does your approach complement or detract from your partner's?

- How can you help each other negotiate individual transitions better?

- How would you change things this year to enhance the time you have together?

Set time aside to go somewhere that you both find relaxing and pleasant and talk about the character traits you have exhibited or seen in each other and those you'd like to exhibit in the coming year.

Make a <u>h</u>allah together.

- As you are cooking, discuss:

  - A time when you wished you'd paused to savor the moment;

  - A time when you or your partner managed to transform a rather ordinary or even disappointing moment into one of shared sweetness or joy.

- As you feed each other <u>h</u>allah dipped in honey, share with each other:

  - Something that you believe helps sustain your relationship.

  - Something that you believe added sweetness to your relationship near its beginning and something that has added sweetness to it more recently.

Learning with a Partner/<u>Hevruta</u>

Experience teaches us that to love is not to gaze at one another but to gaze together in the same direction.

—Antoine de Saint-Exupery

Questions for Discussion

1. Do you find this notion meaningful?

2. When do you choose to gaze into each other's eyes?

3. When you do, what does it say about your love?

4. When have you found that you have looked outward together?

5. Have your ways of doing this changed over time?

6. In what ways would you like to engage in these activities during the coming year?

Do not separate yourself from the community!

—Pirkei Avot 2:4

Questions for Discussion

1. Define community. What does it mean for you?

2. Is your natural inclination to draw near to communities or to separate yourself from them?

3. What things drive you away from communities?

4. What do you see as the benefits of being part of a community?

Human beings need but one book in their life,
When my whole life is gathered like an open book
Before my eyes, when I read it page by page

Seeing with my own eyes how day has followed day,
Flown like page has followed page
In the open book before my eyes.

—Amir Gilboa

Questions for Discussion

1. What page from your life do you keep reviewing?

2. Does your partner see the page in the same way you do?

3. How can you help each other see the page in the larger context of your lives together?

Reaching Out to Others/*Gemilut Hesed*

Block off time together, a few days a year, to contact your member of Congress and your senators to let them know that they are responsible for the well-being of all Americans.

Become a Big Brother or a Big Sister or a foster grandparent, and let a child know that adults can be "present"; model *Hineini*.

Reconnect with your community:

- Invite friends and neighbors to join you for apples and honey and spend a few hours cleaning up a park, a river, or a school.

- Commit to signing up for or organizing ways of being present for people in a community in which you already participate. Find a way of doing this together, if you can: Drive people to the hospital; attend shiva minyans.

Do an energy audit of your home, a utilities' _heshbon hanefesh_—www.homeenergysaver.lbl.gov gives clear guidelines.

- Check your windows and doors for heat seepage.

- Change your shower heads and toilet mechanisms if they waste water.

- Be more conscientious about turning out lights.

Yom Kippur

Yom Kippur, the Day of Atonement, is the most holy day on the Jewish calendar. Many Jewish adults fast from candlelighting on the eve of the holiday till the final shofar blast twenty-six hours later. Synagogue attendance is at its height. Throughout the day we focus on both communal and personal repentance. Prayers of confession are recited aloud in the plural while individuals engage in private reflection. Rabbis often preach about issues of the day; people are encouraged to consider the moral character of their lives.

On the eve of Yom Kippur, the services begin with a special prayer, *Kol Nidrei* (all vows), chanted in Aramaic. Prayer services fill most, if not all, of the day, including a special service when we recall relatives who have died *(Yizkor)*. (Many people light twenty-four-hour *yahrzeit* [memorial] candles that burn throughout Yom Kippur.) As the day progresses, the tenor of the prayers shifts from solemnity and contrition to hopefulness. It ends with a final blast of the shofar and the breaking of the fast.

CHAPTER SIX

Forgiving and Growing: Yom Kippur

Come back, come back
Even though you have broken your vows
A thousand times
Ours is not a house of despair
Ours is a house of hope.

—Rumi

Why is it so difficult to say, "I'm sorry"? Back in the sixties, the novel *Love Story* popularized the saying, "Love means never having to say you're sorry." People laughed a lot over that line. In reality, love—especially when it leads to building a life together—means having to say you are sorry again and again. So it is not surprising that each Yom Kippur, synagogues are filled to overflowing. Although the liturgy is long, complicated, and often opaque, people sense something important is happening. They come because the questions matter so much. How do we ask for forgiveness? How do we truly forgive someone else? How do we begin again? Yom Kippur offers a context in which couples can think about those questions, a context that puts our individual grievances in an ultimately hopeful perspective. We are reminded that brokenness is part of the package, that our challenge is to grow in character, and that, in the end, there is joy and blessing in the work of repair.

Forgiving

Linguist Deborah Tannen has observed that many men engage the world as individuals in a hierarchical social order. In such a view a person is either one-up or one-down, and life is a struggle to avoid failure. Whether you are male or female, admitting error often feels like a defeat. In a time when both men and women strive for achievement in a competitive world, many of us take what Tannen would call a "male" view of apologizing. We don't want to lose ground. But Yom Kippur puts an entirely different spin on the whole idea of confession. The premise of the day is that we are all inevitably flawed but ultimately forgivable. The assumption of universal imperfection is coupled with the promise of acceptance. What a liberating way to think about a relationship!

Brokenness Is Part of the Package

Echoes of Yom Kippur rituals are found throughout the preparations for a traditional wedding. Bride and groom each immerse in a ritual bath to cleanse away the old and prepare for the new. During the afternoon prayers before the ceremony, they recite the Yom Kippur confession. In addition, bride and groom (in some circles only the groom) refrain from eating or drinking on the day of their wedding, breaking the fast with a sip of wine under the *huppah*. And some grooms choose to wear a *kittel*, the white robe worn by many on Yom Kippur.

It is likely that we started our relationships in a spirit of wholeness and hope, regardless of whether or not we observed these particular rituals at our weddings. We knew that we were ending our old lives as single people; a new entity, our twosome, was being born. By initiating marriage with some of the rituals of Yom Kippur, Jewish tradition prepares us for the ever-present need for introspection and repentance in our relationship. We know that we will err; we know that we will need to return to each other in love. We do this annually and collectively on Yom Kippur as part of the Jewish people; in the cycle of our marriage, we do it as needed—usually not often enough.

The collective Jewish story includes important tales of sin and repair. According to the Torah, the very first couple in the world did not find "marriage" easy, nor did they always behave as they might

A *kittel* is a plain white robe worn at significant times of transition in Jewish life: marriage, burial, Yom Kippur, and, in some communities, at the Pesa<u>h</u> seder. The *kittel* serves as a shroud because of the custom of not making class distinctions among our dead. The same confession of sins is recited prior to one's wedding, before one's death, and during the day on Yom Kippur, adding to the powerful imagery of the symbolic link among all of them.

have wished. Recall the story. Adam and Eve are placed in a situation of beauty, ease, and comfort, but soon create quite a bit of chaos. They both disobey God's order, and Adam blames Eve. The two are exiled from paradise. You can imagine the anger that must have provoked! But they start over together, and make a life for themselves in a new, harsher situation. They have two sons. One son kills the other, and Adam and Eve are faced with trauma, grief, and who knows what kind of regrets and recriminations. Once again they appear to forgive each other and themselves enough to create new life. Adam and Eve recoup, have a third son, and manage to carry on (Genesis 2:4–4:25).

In the Torah, human beings continue to make mistakes—often grievous ones—and the Israelites are not immune from this human tendency. The Rabbis link a story of the Israelites' communal sin to Yom Kippur. God reveals the Torah to Moses on Mount Sinai, yet even as this gift is being given, the people below are rebelling by worshiping a golden calf. Moses returns and angrily smashes the tablets on which are written the Ten Commandments. But that is not the end of the story. Moses goes back up the mountain and renegotiates the arrangements. According to the Talmud, Moses returns with a second set of tablets on the day we mark as Yom Kippur. When the Israelites build an ark to hold the written record of the law, they put in it both the new tablets and the fragments of the shattered ones (*Bava Batra* 14b).

Throughout our lives together, we make promises, we grow angry, we find dreams shattered, we try again. Just as Yom Kippur is about imperfection, so are our long-term committed relationships. At the end of a Jewish wedding, we break a glass. Some say this custom helps us recall what is broken in the world, and reminds us that we will inevitably shatter the wholeness of this bright beginning. Perhaps, like the Israelites in the desert, we can benefit from remembering and treasuring the shards. Some people now literally gather the pieces of the glass and work them into a ritual object, a tabletop sculpture or a mezuzah, for instance. Even if we do not save the shards, it is good to remember that brokenness is part of the package. Some things are never fully mended, and that is to be expected. We have room in our hearts and homes for all of it.

What We Can Change and What We Cannot

Each morning Molly's husband, Herb, woke up first and read the newspaper, leaving it in a mess on the table when he was finished. Molly repeatedly asked him to refold it so she could read it with the front page first. Her unsuccessful nagging just made her feel worse. One day she had a revelation: She *did* have options. She could continue each morning looking at the messy paper and thinking, "Herb doesn't really love me!" She could also subscribe to her own newspaper and read it any way she liked. Ultimately, she chose a third path. She decided to make a morning ritual of folding up the paper while meditating on all the ways her sloppy husband *did* show his love for her.

Yom Kippur asks us to confront what we *can* change in our lives—and what we cannot. At the heart of the Yom Kippur liturgy is the image of the Book of Life. Since Rosh Hashanah, our fates have hung in the balance: Will we live or die in the year to come? By the close of Yom Kippur, the traditional liturgy tells us, the Book is sealed, along with our fates. For those who do not believe in a God who sits with open books or who manipulates cancer cells and car accidents, this image serves as a metaphor for a truth about life: Some things are beyond our control. For all that we can do to alter them, many of life's contingencies might just as well have been written in a book by a God in the sky.

Beyond the image of the Book of Life—the decrees we cannot alter—the Yom Kippur liturgy goes on to declare that there are things we do have the power to affect. After listing the various ways we might die in the year to come, it says, "But prayer, repentance, and righteous giving can mitigate the harshness of the decree." Here we are offered some latitude; we don't need to feel stuck. We can choose to pray, to change our thinking, to try to bring more justice to the world. We can choose how to live and how to view what happens to us. We have options. We can still be the authors our lives, or at least author some of the meanings in them.

Ida and Sarah faced the worst pain that could befall parents—the death of their child. They were already in their early sixties when their daughter, the mother of two young daughters, died of breast cancer. In the years immediately surrounding their daughter's illness and death, Ida and Sarah were so involved in the logistics of caring for their daughter and her family that they did not notice what was happening to their own relationship. When they finally stopped focusing on their daughter, Ida and Sarah realized that their bond with each other was seriously frayed. They knew that the statistics were not in their favor. When couples face such a loss, each partner sees the ever-present pain in the other's eyes, sometimes interpreting it as an accusation, sometimes just too unbearable to look at every day; in many cases, one or both opts for escape. But Ida and Sarah chose to work as hard for themselves as they had to help their daughter. They decided to raise money for breast cancer research by participating in a three-day long-distance walk. Their daily training was a physical challenge but as they walked together each morning, they were able to use the time to return to each other. For Ida and Sarah, this became their version of prayer, repentance, and righteous giving.

In our relationships there is an elegant simplicity to discerning what we can change and what we cannot. As a rule, what we can change is our own attitudes and behaviors. What we cannot change is our partners' attitudes and behaviors. Once we realize that our partners will be unlikely to change just because we want them to, we can focus on the prayer, repentance, and righteous giving that is within our own control.

As she entered her forties, Bea became increasingly concerned about health—her own, and her husband's as well. She grew enthusiastic about the idea of diet and exercise. She told Nathan all about it, and she announced that together they would begin a new life regime. Nathan balked. Bea whined, nagged, and lectured. She sent him e-mails with articles about heart disease. She told him that when he exercised, endorphins would kick in, and he would feel so good he would not be able to stop. Nathan didn't buy it. One Yom Kippur afternoon, it dawned on Bea that she was neglecting the one thing she really could control. From then on, she turned her attention to her own diet and exercise program and ceased talking to Nathan about his. The quality of their lives improved immediately. Bea worked out and lost weight, eventually reaching her own goals for herself and feeling good in the process. In due time, when he was ready, Nathan did the same.

Bruce faced a very different challenge. His wife Lydia had a long-time addiction to alcohol. While her addiction did not prevent her from marrying and maintaining a career, it did impair her ability to be emotionally and spiritually present for Bruce. For years, taking his cue from the Yom Kippur liturgy, he thought the situation was one he just had to accept as God's "harsh decree." He was right in thinking he could not change Lydia. But at some point, he realized that he could change his own response. He started to attend meetings of Al-Anon. Eventually, after much soul-searching and the realization that Lydia had no desire or intention to address her addiction, Bruce made another change, and left the marriage. In a case of addiction or abuse, the same rule applies as in any other situation—as a partner you can only change yourself. Sometimes, change in one person begets change in another; but sometimes, it does not, and the only choice left is to move on.

Remembering Those Who Have Died

"There is a land of the living and a land of the dead," wrote Thornton Wilder. During *Yizkor*, the memorial service on Yom Kippur day, the border between those two lands is more open than usual. Three other times during the year *Yizkor* is said to memorialize parents, siblings, partners, and children, but *Yizkor* on Yom Kippur is particularly intense. Thinking about those we have lost is especially challenging at a time of soul-searching and moral accounting.

Death ends lives, but not relationships. In remembering those who are gone, we can't help but remember our unfinished business with them. Sometimes we realize that something is holding us back in our relationship, even though it has nothing directly to do with our partner. It may be that we need to be forgiven by someone who is no longer alive. Or we need to forgive someone but cannot, since they have died. We know that we will not be able to fully be the partner we want to be until we have dealt with this old business.

Yom Kippur is an excellent time to address those things that seem beyond our ability to fix. "The most unnoticed of all miracles is the miracle of repentance," wrote A. J. Heschel. "It is not the same thing as rebirth; it is transformation, creation. In the dimension of time, there is no going back. But the power of repentance causes time to be created backward and allows recreation of the past to take place." On what level can we believe that?

Deborah, recently married for a second time, had been divorced many years before. She had often thought—especially during Yom Kippur—of trying to get together with her ex-husband to talk through old wounds. She knew there were things she would do differently if she had them to do again. Although she had reached the point where she felt ready to tell her ex and ask his forgiveness, she never actually had. When he died—quite suddenly—she found herself mourning both the lost opportunities of her first marriage and the chance to make amends. She explained to her new husband that this year *Yizkor* would be a time when she would have to be alone. She had work to do.

What if we cannot let go of our own anger? Holding a grudge, it is said, is like giving up space in your soul without receiving rent. What a burden we impose on ourselves! A young man once turned to a wise teacher for help with an anger he could not shake. The teacher told him that he had to carry a brick around with him wherever he went for a week. At the end of the week, he was exhausted. "Let it go," the teacher said. "It is a heavy load for you. Just let it go." Yom Kippur helps us find a place of surrender where we will be able to lay down our anger or disappointments and move forward. It provides a statute of limitations on resentment. If the past can be re-made only by the miracle of repentance, the future can still be created by our own efforts. On Yom Kippur, *Yizkor* reminds us that ultimately we will be the ones being remembered.

On Yom Kippur we are either literally or figuratively wearing our shroud, remembering our dead and listening to sermons about what really matters. In 2001 the rabbis' Yom Kippur messages were preempted. A few weeks before the holiday, on September 11, people—those about to jump to their deaths from burning towers and those watching from the safety of their homes—called those most important to them to say, "I love you." Yom Kippur reminds us that we should not wait for national disaster to strike before we express our deepest feelings.

Shawn and Ira routinely attended the services their community held in the homes of members who were mourning a close relative. They both believed this was an important act of *hesed*, loving-kindness, one that made them feel good and made an immediate difference in the lives of others. They noticed that whenever they returned from one of these services, they felt more appreciative of each other, and they fought less. Hearing about the life of someone who was gone reminded them of the difference between what was truly important and what was trivial. Remembering that someday they would be the ones being remembered also helped center them and draw them closer to each other.

Growing

Being human is an accomplishment like playing an instrument. It takes practice.

—Michael Ignatieff

Yom Kippur directs our attention to our ethical behavior. This activity is not restricted to this season of the year, but it is heightened at this time.

As loving partners, we can be each others coaches as we try to grow in *menschlichkeit*. Sylvia was disturbed by her own tendency to gossip and to put down other people, even lightly, when they were not around. One of the places where she was most likely to do this was on the kitchen telephone while working on chores and simultaneously chatting. She shared with her husband her resolve to gossip less in the year to come. He wrote and framed a poster that quoted Proverbs 31—"On her tongue is the law of kindness"—and gave it to her as a gift. They hung it right by the telephone!

Dick wanted to make a major change for the New Year. He saw himself as wasting too much time. He agreed that he needed time for renewal, but when work was hard, particularly when there were challenges he did not want to face, he would while away the entire evening playing solitaire on the computer, watching television, or just daydreaming. He called it "multi-shirking." It felt to him like a moral failing, squandering the precious gift of time. So he asked Norma for help. She agreed that she would sit with him and help him plan his evening: an hour for really pleasurable relaxing, an hour for serious work. And she would be there to help him enforce it, giving him loving words of support along the way.

Rebuke and Apology

We don't have to "call each other" on everything. Justice Ruth Bader Ginsburg recalls the best gift she ever received. It was the night before her wedding, and her mother-in-law-to-be came up to her room and handed her a package. When she unwrapped it, the future associate justice of the Supreme Court found a simple pair of earplugs. "In every good marriage," this wise woman advised, "it pays sometimes to be a little deaf."

But we can't always be deaf. Sometimes we need to tell our partner what is hurting us and request change. The *Mussar* tradition provides rules concerning how and when to rebuke someone who is going astray, recognizing that it takes enormous skill to do it well. How do you best let your partner know when he owes you an apology? Each of us learns over time when and how our partner will be most likely to hear our concerns and suggestions for change positively. And we learn too that it is easier to accept a criticism when it is presented as a reminder of our best selves, our own highest values and stated intentions for our behavior.

We all like to hear "I am sorry," but for some people it is very hard to say. The best apology goes something like this: "I am so sorry I hurt you. I see now exactly why what I did would make you feel bad. I also see how I ended up doing what I did. It is clear to me how next time around I can plan ahead and make a better choice. I promise I will try my best to do so."

Many of us will wait our whole lives to hear an apology like that from our partners. It is the gold standard. Serena's partner Arthur could manage bits of it, on different occasions, but his apologies never lived up to her expectations. She would insist on more. "I know you are sorry, but do you *really* understand why I am mad?

A branch of literature in Jewish tradition known as *Mussar*, literally "tradition" but popularly understood to mean character education, focuses on ethical behavior and the virtues we need to become the people we are meant to be. Some texts have become classics, read and studied lovingly for hundreds of years. The great masters of *Mussar* agreed that the reason we were each put on this earth was to become a *mensch*, Yiddish for a genuine human being.

In the nineteenth century, the *Mussar* movement in Lithuania, headed by Rabbi Israel Salanter, encouraged Jewish men to devote themselves to ethical improvement. They spent many hours in their houses of study, hunched over books in pairs, working on character development through the study of *Mussar* texts.

Are you *really* sure you have figured out how to do better?" At this point, Arthur would shut down or angrily retract his apology. Over the years, she came to realize that admitting wrong was not an easy thing, and she trained herself to be grateful for the efforts he made to let her know he was sorry. She never heard everything she hoped to hear, but she appreciated that he was giving it his best effort.

Two rabbis once watched a colleague collecting money for communal funds from a notorious miser. They noticed that he offered profuse thanks, even for a stingy contribution, given reluctantly. "We would have thrown that penny back in his face! Why do you shower him with praise? And why do you keep after him so patiently?" they wondered. Later that day, the rabbi showed them the additional funds the man had given, explaining, "Bit by bit he came around." We can do the same with our partners as we teach one another how to stumble, apologize (we'll keep getting better at it), and forgive.

Another of the many Shammai and Hillel disputes reminds us of what Rabbi Harold Schulweis calls the "Jewish reality principle." What if someone stole a beam of wood and built it into the structure of his home, and then the theft was discovered? The house of Shammai says that the beam must be returned, even if it means demolishing the home. Hillel says to leave the home in place and pay the worth of the beam (*Mishnah Gittin* 5:5). Hillel's teaching makes a point worth remembering. We need not go back over everything, demolishing as we go. Sometimes things get built in less-than-ideal ways, but we move on. We cannot always make restitution in the place where the fault lies, but we can make it somewhere else.

Second chances

On Yom Kippur we are confronted with the possibility of reversing our direction, no matter how long or how far we have strayed. The possibility of change is inspiring. It is also challenging and often frightening. Some couples engage in the same low-grade quarrel over and over again, for years. Neither of them really knows what they are arguing about, except that it has become their way of interacting. As the years go by, it grows harder to find the energy to make a shift. They are afraid to even try to change, because it will make them feel that they should have done it years ago. If they stay stuck, they feel vindicated in thinking that their failure is inevitable. They find comfort in the familiar; at least they know the routine.

One evening Beth and Glen were invited to dinner with their daughter, her husband, and their granddaughter, Julie. They hardly ever got to see their granddaughter, and they were thrilled. As the evening progressed, Beth and Glen began to quarrel with each other, as they frequently did. Halfway through the meal, their daughter beckoned to Beth to follow her into the kitchen. "Mom," she said. "You and Dad have to cut it out! I don't want Julie subjected to this. If you can't be nicer to each other, I really don't want you to visit." Shocked, Beth made it through the next hour and then hustled Glen out the door. As they drove home, Beth told Glen what their daughter had said. They both stared into the dark night. Finally, Beth broke the silence. "I know it's late in the game, but I want to try to work on our relationship. Will you give it a chance?"

Sometimes something happens that forces us to ask ourselves God's question to Adam: "Where are you?" And the answer we hear is: "The place where I am standing is not where I want to be." Sometimes, we are ready to move on, never mind the regrets. At those moments, we can remember the *Sheheheyanu* blessing: We are alive, we have made it to this time, we have been sustained, and we will always be able to enjoy this gift, the blessing of the second chance.

Moving Forward

Community

For centuries Jews have poured the burden of their lives—their sorrows, their aspirations, their moral striving—into Yom Kippur. As we think about all the courage that has been brought to this day over time—all the hearts broken with remorse, all the willingness to admit wrong, all the openness to forgive—we are buoyed in our belief that we too can move on in our lives. Something powerful emerges from this day that is greater than the sum of its parts.

In the synagogue service, we recount our failures, reciting the *Vidui,* the traditional confessional prayer, first alone in silence and then together aloud. This prayer is written in the first person plural, implying that whatever it is we need, be it solace or strength or rebuke, we cannot find it alone.

Rabbi Joseph Soloveitchik reports that in Europe the old men would weep as they recited the *Vidui* silently, each one lost in his own fear and trembling before God as he thought about his own sins and errors. But when the time came for the communal repetition, the tune became more upbeat and the tone more confident. Each held and carried the other's sins. As a community, their collective merits outweighed each other's faults. Together they were strong, even bold. They tapped into the accumulated power of their shared willingness to carry one another's burdens.

Taking that back into our year, we realize how powerful it is to be surrounded by others. From the twelve-step programs, to Weight Watchers, to Rosh Hodesh groups for women, we can see the power of groups in helping people as they work toward difficult goals. Some couples have found that this insight can apply to their partnership as well.

When Nina and Ben faced new challenges as their aging

parents became more dependent, they turned to a small group of friends and created a "couples group." Once a month they met and shared issues, setbacks, and triumphs. Each confessed that they had hoped their relationship would be like a "self-cleaning oven," but discovered along the way that sometimes they needed to take out the scouring pads. As at Yom Kippur, the presence of others with similar struggles gave them strength.

Groups like this have met to study texts (from the Bible to the latest marriage guides), view videos, check in on each other's progress, or just have fun. Such a group can also celebrate the blessing of having a community with which to share issues. It might be organized around a life cycle theme such as "Recent Empty Nesters" or it might benefit from including couples at different stages in life. You could create such a group at your synagogue or through another community to which you belong. Some groups are led by rabbis or another trained person, and others are not. Some people who would never join a support group might sign up for a class with a rabbi and end up doing some sharing, despite themselves. Like Nina and Ben, you could just bring together couples you know who value companions on their journey.

The Blessing of the Work

Before we eat, Jewish tradition tells us to take a minute and offer a blessing, a pause that allows us to acknowledge the gratitude we feel for what we are about to receive. Yom Kippur is a daylong pause, a "blessing" if you will, before the year to come. We don't know what the year will bring, but we know we need to fan the tiny sparks inside ourselves that will grow into a soul strong and sensitive enough to handle whatever may come along with courage and grace.

Yom Kippur is not an altogether solemn day. A Hasid was once heard singing as he left for the *Kol Nidrei* service. His disciple asked, "How can you be so happy? The service you are about to attend is very, very hard. You need to confront what is most painful

and most flawed in your life. Why are you singing?" He replied,
"The man who sweeps the dirt out of the royal palace is happy as
he works, for he knows he is toiling in the home of a king."

On Yom Kippur, we sense that the "dirty" work of looking
hard at our failings, sweeping out the dust from last year, becomes
sacred work. Wherever we do this becomes a sacred palace. It is
this intention that we can take into our year—what an honor it
is to have a life to work on and improve! And as couples, we can
experience the privilege of having a relationship to repair as
well. When we think of the Hasid singing as he works, we can
try to capture or enhance a sense of the joy and privilege of
working to become the subjects of our lives.

At the end of Yom Kippur, after the closing prayers of the
holiday service, we chant the evening prayers for a regular weekday because … well, because life goes on. It is time to chant the
evening prayers, including the regular prayer for forgiveness, even
though we have not had time to get into any kind of trouble at all!
Already we are repenting again. And so the tradition reminds us,
as we embark on the New Year, of the persistence of imperfection.
This message can be encouraging: We will never be perfect, but,
like generations before us, we bring hope to each new year, each
new day.

When Yom Kippur is over, traditional Jews go home and,
after a quick meal to break the fast, get out the hammer and start
work on the *sukkah*, the makeshift structure that will provide a
temporary home for the next holiday. Yom Kippur teaches us to
humbly accept our limitations as human beings and, after all the
breast-beating is complete, get back to work. When we are lucky,
we have someone by our side to hold the ladder and hand over
the nails.

Celebrations/*Minhagim*

Write a letter to each other, stating your hopes for your own behavior in the year to come and how you believe your partner can best support you in realizing your goals.

Try to spend the afternoon before *Kol Nidrei* immersing together in water. This could be in a natural body of water (weather permitting), a swimming pool, a hot tub, a bathtub, or —as a last resort—a home shower. Discuss with each other:

- What needs to be washed away from the year that has passed.

- How you can help each other enter the New Year clean. (This is a ritual that can work for you as a couple at any time of year, at any moment when it is appropriate for you to have your own personal Yom Kippur.)

Light candles to usher in the holiday at sunset, including *yahrzeit* candles for relatives who have died.

- You might want to place their photos next to the candles.

- Recount the blessings of their lives, ask their forgiveness, and bless each other for the year to come.

Learning with a Partner/<u>H</u>evruta

Rava said: "On the day you are entered into judgment you will be asked six questions:
Did you deal faithfully [i.e., with integrity], did you fix times for learning, did you engage in procreation, did you hope for salvation, did you engage in the dialectics of wisdom, did you understand one thing from another?"

—*Shabbat* 31a

Questions for Discussion

1. Are these the questions you would have guessed would be asked "at heaven's gates"?

2. Which ones seem surprising to you?

3. What seems to be left out?

4. Can you answer these questions for yourself with regard to the year that just passed?

5. How might you help each other answer them in the year to come?

The *Mussar* literature contains lists of virtues *(middot)* that we should work to cultivate in ourselves. Examine this traditional list:

> *Wisdom, Trustworthiness, Loving-kindness,*
> *Common Decency, Compassion, Zeal, Generosity,*
> *Wealth, Charity, Humility, Modesty, Contentedness,*
> *Inclining toward Good, Shamefacedness, Will, Pure-*
> *Heartedness, A Good Name, Peace, Observing*
> *Commandments, Repentance, Prayer, Knowing God,*
> *Fearing God, Loving God.*

> —*Sefer Maalot HaMiddot*

Questions for Discussion

1. Do you agree that all of these are virtues you would want to pursue?

2. Why or why not?

3. Can you each identify two virtues you plan to explore as a couple through text study?

For two and a half years, the School of Shammai and the School of Hillel debated one issue. Would it have been better for human beings not to have been created? Finally, they voted and it was decided: It would have been better for human beings not to have been created. However, now that they have been, let them examine their deeds.

—*Eruvin* 13a

Questions for Discussion

1. Which side would you take in this debate?

2. Does it make a difference which side you believe?

Reaching Out/*Gemilut Hesed*

The words of Isaiah read on Yom Kippur say that fasting will have been in vain if it does not inspire action. In this spirit, donate a day's worth of food to a hunger relief organization, whether or not you fast on Yom Kippur. Mazon: A Jewish Response to Hunger allocates donations from the Jewish community to prevent and alleviate hunger among people of all backgrounds. See www.mazon.org.

In remembering a parent, beloved relative, or friend who has died, recall a particular mitzvah that this individual undertook, or one that would be especially relevant to their life, either in terms of their values or the challenges they faced. Commit yourself to doing that mitzvah in their name during the coming year.

If you are both able to, make a commitment to give blood together on the *yahrzeits* that either or both of you observe.

Sukkot

Sukkot is the autumn harvest festival. Its origins are biblical and, like Shavuot, it was celebrated by making a pilgrimage to the Temple in Jerusalem and offering God the fruits of the season. It also commemorates the forty years that the Jews wandered in the desert and dwelt in temporary shelters, or booths, known as *sukkot*. Many Jews and Jewish communities erect a *sukkah*, a temporary booth, and gather with family and friends to eat and sometimes sleep in it during this weeklong festival.

The *sukkah* is decorated with seasonal fruits and plants, and pictures and prayers are put on the walls. The rituals of Sukkot include blessing and shaking the *lulav* (willow, myrtle, and palm branches bound together) and *etrog* (citron), all indigenous to Israel, as symbols of the ancient harvest. To underscore the heightened joy of this first festival after the lengthy contemplation of the High Holy Days, Sukkot is also known as the "season of our joy," *zeman simhateinu*.

There are two main blessings associated with the holiday. Upon entering a *sukkah* we say: *Barukh atah Adonai, Eloheinu Melekh haolam, asher kidshanu b'mitzvotav v'tzivanu leisheiv ba-sukkah;* We praise you, God, Source of Life, who makes us holy with your mitzvot and commands us to sit in the *sukkah*. While holding the *lulav* and *etrog*, prior to shaking them, we say: *Barukh atah Adonai, Eloheinu Melekh haolam, asher kidshanu b'mitzvotav v'tzivanu al n'tilat lulav;* We praise you, God, Source of Life, who makes us holy with your mitzvot and commands us to wave the *lulav*. In addition, on the first day we add the *Sheheheyanu* (see page 14).

CHAPTER SEVEN

Blessing Bounty, Facing Impermanence: Sukkot

To live in this world
you must be able
to do three things:
to love what is mortal;
to hold it
against your bones knowing
your own life depends on it;
and, when the time comes to let it go,
to let it go.

—Mary Oliver

The *sukkah* is tiny and inconsequential as it stands in the openness of the universe, or, as it originally did, in the vastness of the desert that the ancient Jews crossed. And yet, like a palm tree in a storm, this fragile structure withstands the vagaries of seasonal change—scorching heat, cool nights, driving wind and rain. It symbolizes both the bounty and the frailty of the created world. It embodies the paradoxical truth that, in nature, growth can occur only when it coexists with death and decay.

A sukkah is constructed to last for one week, based on the biblical statement: "You shall observe it as a festival of Adonai for seven days in the year; you shall observe it in the seventh month as a law for all time, throughout the ages. You shall live in booths seven days; all citizens in Israel shall live in booths, in order that future generations may know that I brought them out of the land of Egypt, I Adonai your God" (Leviticus 23:41–43).

The *sukkah* is a reminder that to be alive is to change, and that everything that lives must die. Constructed to last for just one week, its existence is finite. It offers beauty, respite, and peace, but not eternity.

Blessing Bounty

How much richer our life as a couple would be if we internalized Sukkot's message of gratitude for both the ephemeral and the enduring. While our relationships last far more than a week, they are not eternal. We build them and fortify them to be a constant source of beauty, comfort, and sanctity in our lives. Yet we cannot ignore reality: Relationships can end for many reasons, and we cannot assume that we will *always* be by one another's side. Sometimes, this knowledge is overwhelming and frightening. Most of the time, we somehow manage to get through the crises of our lives, and move forward even when we believe we can't. We transform uncertainty and change—sources of fear and trepidation—into reasons for rejoicing, expressing gratitude for what has been and for what is, and hope for what may yet be. We "decorate our relationship *sukkah*" with the fruits of today, so that we may savor the present moment. We believe that our existence is enriched by taking life's greatest risk—to love—despite the knowledge that the loss of that love will surely be painful.

Sensuality and Living Fully

At Sukkot we are told to take hold of the things that we have harvested, that we know will not grow again for some time. We are told to feel them, to look at their size and shape, to smell them and savor their fragrance. We decorate the *sukkah* with the produce of our local harvests, feasting on sights that will soon disappear from the landscape. And we are told to bring into the *sukkah* leaves (*lulav*) and fruit (*etrog*), symbolizing the bounty of the harvest in ancient Israel. As we shake them in all directions, the rustling of the leaves makes music for our ears and the strong, sweet scents fill our lungs and the whole *sukkah*. When we sit down to eat in the *sukkah*, our senses are heightened, and we taste the rich, distinct flavors of everything we put into our mouths. And as we do, we experience a sense of fulfillment, joy, and gratitude that is so powerful we are moved to song. The traditional liturgy adds *Hallel*, songs or psalms of praise, to the synagogue service for this reason.

We are encouraged to savor this moment, to create a multilayered memory, one involving all our senses. After the holiday is over, we will always be able to bring it to mind, to recapture it in our hearts through its special sights, sounds, touch, tastes, and smells.

Ginny enjoys the early morning hours when she lies quietly next to Tracey. She listens to Tracey's short, heavy little breaths; she enjoys the warmth radiating from Tracey's sleeping body. Every so often Ginny's reverie is interrupted and she is gripped by the realization that some day all she will probably have are memories; Tracey won't always be there beside her. Most of the time this flash of awareness recedes as quickly as it came, and she returns to the soft breathing, the unfurrowed brow, the sweet scent, and the abiding joy and desire that the sight of Tracey evokes. She strokes her hair as she sleeps, grateful to be with her.

And sometimes, during the day, she finds herself thinking of those quiet morning hours and momentarily recaptures their smells and sounds and sensations, awash with that joy all over again.

What would it be like to be conscious of touching each thing and each person we encounter with the joy and urgency that comes from knowing we may never have a chance to do so again? What would we say and do differently?

Invitations and Sharing

The *sukkah* is not a structure for solitary sitting. It is a place for rejoicing and affirming life, a place for gathering: gathering the fruits of the field, the signs of our bounty, the people who enrich our lives.

When Bonita and Rafi looked around at the twenty people who had gathered for dinner in their yard during Sukkot, they were overwhelmed. This was the fulfillment of what had once seemed a mere fantasy. Five years ago, as Bonita and Rafi were driving home from a night of volunteering at a local nursing home, they talked about how wonderful it would be for there to be a dependable group of volunteers visiting the residents every night of the week. They spoke to various community groups about the joys they had found in their nursing home work, and slowly they attracted others and began to train them. Now, they rejoiced in what they had created, as they shared a celebratory meal in their *sukkah* with all the nursing home's evening volunteers.

Jewish tradition offers an interesting insight: At the changing of the seasons, at times of reflection or joy, not only do the living gather with us at our tables—the dead join us as well. Often, the absent voices call to us, evoking memories, reminding us of where we've come from, causing us to consider who we are now. An old and chipped candlestick, a long-discolored tallit, the gravy bowl we bring out just for Thanksgiving trigger a flood of memories of those who passed them down. Consciously we choose to take them out, and lovingly we interact with them.

We gather together for meals of celebration and meals of consolation. Our meals of celebration are tinged with nostalgia, recalling times and people who are no longer with us. Our meals of consolation call forth both tears and laughter as we share stories and memories of the one who has died. At Sukkot, as the lush fruits and vegetables of autumn belie the dying stalks and bare trees that once nurtured them, we surround ourselves with those who once nurtured us, remembering the gifts they gave us, the enduring treasures that today help define us and our lives.

The *Zohar* (*Emor* 103a) speaks of inviting seven biblical characters into the *sukkah*.

We can expand this tradition further by inviting our heroes and heroines, living or dead, and even our personal loved ones, by name, to enter our *sukkah*. They can become our honored guests, no longer lurking in the recesses of our dining room, *sukkah*, hearts, or minds, but invited to sit among us, to participate in the conversation and be acknowledged for their contributions to our lives. Another custom is to find photographs of the guests we invite, place them in clear plastic covers, and hang them on the walls of the *sukkah*.

Sukkot begs us to confront the realities of human existence. Our lives are fleeting. Our days

According to the mystical tradition, special guests, known as *ushpizin* (Aramaic for "guests"), are invited into the *sukkah*: Abraham, Isaac, Jacob, Joseph, Moses, Aaron, and David are believed to enter as those in the *sukkah* recite a blessing of welcome. This custom has been expanded in recent years to include women: Sarah, Rebecca, Rachel, Leah, Miriam, Abigail, and Esther, or other notable Jewish women.

are numbered. And none of us knows how long we have to spend with those we love—with their speaking directly to us, smiling at us, shedding tears with and for us, encouraging us, nagging us—being there in the fullness of life, not just in memory.

Vulnerability

The *sukkah*, by definition, is vulnerable. It is made of a few sticks, perhaps some plastic sheeting or cloth to form walls, and a roof of branches open to the sky. Yet inside the *sukkah*, the cold of the outside is mitigated by the warmth of other bodies; the open roof literally allows our songs to rise to the heavens. Sometimes during the week of Sukkot, the branches on the roof must be replaced, and the poles that hold up the walls must be replanted or reinforced. So too it is with our relationships. Circumstances shift and change and we are confronted with reminders of our own fragility. Yet we go on, believing that with the changes something profound and holy endures.

Leslie picked the napkin up off the floor and put it back on Paul's lap. Their eyes met, tenderly conveying their love for one another. Since Paul's arthritis had gotten worse, even bending over had become an ordeal for him. They could both remember when he had only occasional aches and pains in his legs and hips; nothing could stop him then. Now, even retrieving a napkin was too difficult. Over the years, without having to discuss it, they had both altered their movements to accommodate Paul's diminishing physical capabilities. They no longer were able to go out dancing, which they had loved, but Paul continued to make Leslie float as no one else could—yesterday on the dance floor, and still, today, with his smiling eyes and tender voice.

For Carol, her encounter with her own physical vulnerability was abrupt and life-threatening. She had been sitting with friends at dinner. Suddenly she felt a bit distressed, and the next thing she remembered was looking at paramedics in an ambulance. She was hooked up to heart monitors and many other machines; the pain in her chest was oppressive. She was having a heart attack. In fact, many months later, Carol realized that her heart's failure had attacked her entire way of life as well: She was going to have to alter her daily routines, eating habits, and who knew what else.

We let ourselves become lulled into security by our creature comforts and our ability to make decisions about some of the discrete moments of our lives. We often avoid the message contained in Ecclesiastes (traditionally read on the Sabbath during Sukkot) that the joys of today may not be ours tomorrow and that, ultimately, little is under our control. And we continue to live as if we can control our lives. Many of us still find open communication about end-of-life matters exceedingly difficult. We each hold our own views about the nature and meaning of life and death. And while we may think that our partner understands how we feel about palliative care, euthanasia, burial, organ donation, and the like, in the absence of specific conversations together, we are taking a risk that our desires and wishes will not be honored when the time comes.

When his mother had advanced Alzheimer's disease, Ralph had commented to Celia over and over again that he never wanted to be kept alive were he to be in that condition; he never wanted to be a "living vegetable." When family members and friends had suggested they get living wills and advance directives, they simply said they knew what each of them wanted; an attorney didn't need to write it all out. Then Celia got the call from an out-of-state hospital that Ralph had been in a major car accident. The nurse explained that he had serious head injuries, needed surgery, and there was no guarantee that he would regain his mental capacities. The nurse asked Celia to fax them Ralph's advance directive; Celia said she could tell them what her husband wanted. The nurse said that wasn't enough; they needed it in writing.

In the sacred context of the holiday of Sukkot, at a time when we are most aware of the bounty of our lives, perhaps we can muster the courage to sit down and do the painful work of acknowledging our own mortality and the mortality of our partner. We need to address our own fragility and share with our loved ones our concerns and desires pertaining to end-of-life decisions. We can create living wills and advance directives together, and legally ensure that our wishes will be followed. We can choose to designate someone other than our spouse as the decision-maker if we know that it will be too painful for our partner to have to articulate that ultimate decision. We can put in writing our desires related to death and burial. We can fill out the necessary forms for organ donation and give permission for autopsy, or explicitly refuse them. Relieving family members of the stress of having to make decisions at a time of heightened anxiety or grief can be an act of great love, one that will be cherished long after we are gone. The joy of Sukkot or another significant moment can ballast the trepidation that might otherwise prevent us from preparing these important documents.

Every year at Sukkot, Harry and Alice take each other's hand as they approach their *sukkah*, in exactly the same way they approached their ḥuppah. They pause just inside the door and share with each other one thing that has changed significantly in the past year, and one thing they did together that helped them get through the change more comfortably. They then offer a blessing, thanking God for having each other in their lives. Perhaps in a *sukkah*, perhaps at another significant threshold you cross infrequently (for example, a place where you vacation), you can engage in a similar ritual, and utter a similar prayer or other words such as these:

O my love, O my love we dance
under the <u>h</u>uppah standing over us
like an animal on its four legs,
like a table on which we set our love
as a feast, like a tent
under which we work
not safe but no longer solitary
in the searing heat of our time.

—*Marge Piercy*

Celebrations/*Minhagim*

Go to a part of your home where you feel most secure and discuss:

- A time in the last year when you felt most vulnerable.

- The structures you have put in place to increase your sense of protection and safety.

- A moment of uncertainty or change that you now look back on with joy or gratitude.

Invite those who contributed to your life into your *sukkah* and tell them why you asked them to come (if you are not in a *sukkah*, you can do this at the dinner table).

When you and your partner have time to relax and enjoy each other's company, focus on one part of your partner's body:

- Imagine it in as much detail as you can.

- Explore that part of your partner's body, with all of your senses, so you will later have a variety of ways to bring it to mind.

During an anticipated period of relaxation—Shabbat, a long weekend, a vacation, a time of repose and plentitude—plan for a future that will reflect who you are.

- Begin by expressing gratitude.

- Reflect with each other about the losses that scare you the most.

- If you do not already have living wills, health care proxies, or advance directives, talk with each other about preparing them.

- If you do have living wills, health care proxies, or advance directives, review them. If your thoughts about any of the details have changed, take steps to modify them.

- Express gratitude for having articulated clearly your wishes and expectations and for gaining greater understanding about what your partner wishes and expects.

Learning with a Partner/_Hevruta_

> Teach us how short our time is
>   let us know it in the depths of our souls
> Show us that all things are transient
>   as insubstantial as dreams
> and that after heaven and earth have vanished
>   there is only you.
> Fill us in the morning with your wisdom
>   shine through us all our lives
> Let our hearts soon grow transparent
>   in the radiance of your love

Show us how precious each day is;
  teach us to be fully here.
And let the work of our hands
  prosper, for our little while.

—Stephen Mitchell

Questions for Discussion

1. What have you done to address your concerns about the future?

2. What gives you comfort in the face of life's fragility?

To everything there is a season
And a time to every purpose under heaven.
A time to be born
A time to die
A time to plant
A time to reap
A time to kill
A time to heal
A time to weep
A time to laugh
A time to wail
A time to dance.

—Ecclesiastes 3:1–4

Questions for Discussion

1. What meaning do these words have for you and your relationship?

2. What season would you say your relationship is in at the present?

3. Which seasons have you already experienced?

4. What are your strongest memories of each of those seasons?

People associate love with sentimental feeling alone. But love includes much more. The act of love should bring all levels of the human being into play, his intuitions, his emotions, and his logic and mind as well.

—Rav Kuk

Questions for Discussion

1. How has your partner helped you bring your intuitions, emotions, logic, and mind into play?

2. Which of these areas do you wish you could find further expression for?

3. How can your partner help you bring more parts of yourself into your life together?

Reaching Out/*Gemilut Hesed*

Make your home safer and more secure:

• Child-proof your home.

• Install fire alarms and check them regularly.

• Make entrances to your home accessible.

• Make sure your stairs, decks, roof, and walks are well maintained.

Learn more about Jewish practices related to death and burial, and consider joining a lay Jewish burial society (_hevrah kadisha_). Visit www.jewish-funerals.org for more information.

Visit those who are not as strong, vigorous, or healthy as you are in hospitals, nursing homes, hospices, or rehabilitation facilities.

Simhat Torah

During the course of the year, the Torah is read from beginning to end, with prescribed consecutive sections read each week and special portions read on holidays. On Simhat Torah (Rejoicing in the Torah), the final portion—the reading of the last chapters of Deuteronomy—is followed by the opening chapters of Genesis, symbolizing the commitment to ongoing Torah study.

Simhat Torah comes on the day after the conclusion of Sukkot and brings to an end the intensive holiday season that began with Elul. After Simhat Torah, there is a lull in the calendar until Hanukkah.

Communities often honor special individuals by calling them to the Torah on this day, and this is the one day in the year when children are also called to the Torah. Many communities read from only one Torah scroll; in order to begin the cycle again, they roll the Torah from its end to its beginning. Others read from two separate scrolls. In any event, Jews take this opportunity to parade around the synagogue with the Torah(s), singing and dancing.

CHAPTER EIGHT

Committing to the Process: Sim*h*at Torah

As the Torah scroll is read aloud each year ...
So we two roll together
And every year our love gets a new reading.

—Yehuda Amichai

Week after week, year after year, century after century, the Jewish people have been circling the seasons with the Torah. One might expect Sim*h*at Torah, which is all about commitment to the Torah, to be a serious holiday in the yearly cycle. Instead, it is characterized by zest and mirth. Amidst dancing, parades, and parodies, the Torah cycle officially ends and begins again. This anniversary celebration has much to teach us as couples. We learn about commitment and joy, the intimacy of shared learning, and the marking of the seasons in our own lives.

Commitment and Joy

Commitment is hard work. The twentieth-century poet Rainier Maria Rilke called marriage "day labor." Sim*h*at Torah celebrates commitment. It rests on the assumption that each year we will roll back the Torah scrolls and begin the annual cycle of readings once more, despite any ambivalence we may have. Imagine if one year we said, "Enough of this Torah story! Next year let's read Shakespeare!" Or, "Enough of this God who has let us down more times than not this year. Why not say this relationship has been through enough, and we are moving on?" Commitment may be arduous labor, but the signature virtue of this holiday is not diligence but joy. Simhat Torah reminds us that along with the day labor is the dance.

Just as on Shavuot, wedding imagery suffuses the celebration of Simhat Torah. This time, however, the themes are different. On Shavuot the focus is on vows and pledges, on rules and expectations. Here, the emphasis is on the pure joy of being together. On Shavuot we stay up all night studying; on Simhat Torah we stay up rejoicing, dancing, and singing. We have been through a lot together. It is time to put an exuberant exclamation point on the year.

The synagogue service on Simhat Torah is the occasion for a playful wedding of sorts. The Torah is marched around the synagogue seven times to represent the seven circuits a bride takes around her groom under the *huppah*, the marriage canopy, in traditional Jewish weddings. Then congregants hold aloft a mock *huppah*, and children enter and are blessed. In traditional synagogues two men are honored with the title of *hatan*, bridegroom of the Torah, which is the bride in this little drama. In the old villages of Eastern Europe, the women sometimes had their own celebration and crowned the rabbi's wife *kallah*, bride of the Torah. In liberal synagogues today everyone celebrates together, and the honorees are usually of both sexes.

Marriage manuals promise that you will "learn new skills," become competent at "fighting fair," and practice "listening exercises." All this may be helpful, but it sometimes starts to sound about as inviting as eating oat bran straight from the box. While earnest suggestions such as "Schedule a meeting to discuss areas of trust and mistrust" might be useful in some cases, they tend to focus our attention on problems and difficulties. Simḥat Torah suggests that "working on your relationship" is only part of the picture. Like the Jews' commitment to the Torah, your long-term engagement with your partner is a joy to be celebrated.

The love affair of the Jews with the Torah reminds us as well that argument can be part of the joy. There are parts of the Torah whose wisdom we hold dear and parts we argue against passionately. As we read each Torah portion, we debate with the text, with interpreters from the past, and with each other. The "god-wrestle" (as Arthur Waskow calls it) that is Torah study is a model for placing differences in perspective. This positive spin on disputation is not limited to Torah study. An elderly Jewish woman, an immigrant from Eastern Europe living in a poor community in Los Angeles, explained to an anthropologist, "We fight to keep warm."

Keeping It New

In a culture that glorifies what is new, a long-term committed relationship is something of a challenge. You may have heard someone say jokingly, "I've been married to four or five different women and I never even had to get a divorce." Usually the person is referring to the way people change over a lifetime and how, if we are so blessed, we can stay married to one person through each of these incarnations. But the deeper meaning is that at any moment we can encounter each other in multiple ways, on multiple levels.

How is it that the study of Torah does not eventually become stale? The answer lies in the many layers that readers uncover in the text. Jewish tradition speaks about four levels of meaning in any statement in the Torah—the literal (*pshat*), allusion (*remez*), homiletic/explanatory (*drash*), and mystical (*sod*). The initial letters of each of these words in Hebrew together spell the word, PaRDeS, which means paradise. Human beings can also be seen as multilayered "texts." Rabbi Dayle Friedman suggests that chaplains look and listen to the person before them on many levels simultaneously; we can do the same in our most intimate relationships.

Your partner comes home and shares a story about something that happened at work. You can listen on many levels. On the level of plain text, the story is about who said what to whom, where, and when. And you can respond by finding out more details. But then there is the level of allusion. This involves reading between the lines or listening between the words. What is your partner's tone of voice? How is she sitting as she talks? What are the unspoken clues to what this story might mean beyond the plain sense, the plot that would be recorded in a police report? Then there is the explanation. What does this story mean to your partner in the context of her life? Her values? What kind of interpretation is she bringing to what she describes? The same statement, "I didn't get a raise this year," can mean very different things depending on the meanings your partner attributes to money, authority, or professional life. Investigate.

Finally, there is the mystical, the level that can barely be spoken of but the level that is about the soul. This level requires us to be present in the deepest possible way. Our evolved human brains, the parts that no other animal shares, are busy at work when we listen to the plain text and seek out explanations. But there is a level of connection that goes beyond words; this kind of encounter cannot be planned for, only experienced and appreciated.

Shared Learning

As the student in the movie *Shadowlands* says to C.S. Lewis, "We read to know we are not alone." He probably means that we can find friends in the characters in books. The Torah is a book that is meant to be read over and over as a companion to our lives. And, perhaps most important, we do not expect to be alone when we read it; we read it together with someone else. Couples can find a surprising intimacy in reading any book to each other. The psychiatrist Robert Coles recalls that his parents read out loud to each other. "Your mother and I feel rescued by these books," the elder Coles explained.

Larry had grown up in a Jewish family while Ann had been raised Catholic. Larry was so little connected to his Judaism that he was willing to be married by a priest for the sake of Ann's family. But Ann was not comfortable with Catholicism, so they were married by a Unitarian minister. They wanted their children to have a religious upbringing, and found a Jewish Community Center to ground the kids in a Jewish identity. When the children got older, Larry and Ann decided to search for some spiritual meaning for themselves. Each began exploring different prayer communities and reading about other religious beliefs. Once a week, they made a practice of sitting down and reading to each other from the books they were each discovering. This sharing of ideas gave them an ongoing, vital sense of connection to each other.

Dancing

On Simḥat Torah, we express our joy through our bodies, by dancing with the Torah. Study feels intuitively Jewish to us; glorying in

The statement "If I can't dance, I don't want to be in your revolution!" is attributed to Emma Goldman. Alix Kates Shulman tells the story of how she created this quotation for a feminist T-shirt, basing it on a story in Emma Goldman's 1931 autobiography, in which Goldman said something along these lines, although at much greater length.

physicality and movement seems strange, less familiar. Yet here, at the heart of the final holiday of the cycle of Torah reading, physical exaltation is paired with the book learning of Torah.

Some religious traditions have incorporated movement into their spiritual practices in ways that our modern world is rediscovering to our great benefit and joy. Think of the surge of interest in yoga and tai chi. The more we learn about ourselves, the more we realize that body, mind, and spirit are all deeply connected. The health of one affects the health of the others. Many of us find that we can borrow and blend insights from different traditions to create a path to wholeness.

Our bodies and our senses can also be a path for learning. Some of us are visual learners, some auditory, and some kinesthetic. Sometimes we need to learn in ways that are not our primary mode. How aware are you of your partner's learning style (or, for that matter, your own)? When you are trying to impart something to your partner, do you sometimes become frustrated when he fails to "get it"? You each might want to consciously engage in some learning through one of your less-dominant modes, guided by your partner.

You and your partner may want to discuss this in relation to your spiritual lives. We each find transcendence in different ways. Phil and Brad are both highly kinesthetic, and they avidly pursue sports together with religious passion. Neither would be happy sitting still for long, so they are well matched in their plans for their weekends. In another couple, Stacey is tone deaf and not terribly interested in music. For her, an off-key prayer leader chanting a Jewish service is just fine; she is focused on the words. Barry, on the other hand, is quite musical and finds his own spiritual experiences at good concerts. Realizing the meaning of these concerts in his life, Stacey sometimes comes along. At first it was just to support him, but now she has grown to enjoy them as well.

Living with a partner who opens you to an unfamiliar way of engaging with life provides a great opportunity to learn to grasp the world in different ways. Don't assume that what has served as a path in the past necessarily has to be your only mode in the future. Your soul may open in new ways that surprise you.

Jewish Identity

Sometimes developments in the history of the Jewish people bring about new twists in the evolution of a holiday. In Soviet Moscow, beginning in the 1960s, after decades of being forbidden to practice religion, many Jews acted on their strong desire to embrace and express their Jewish identity. They found a way in an enthusiastic embrace of the holiday of Simhat Torah. Jews began to flood the streets of Moscow on this holiday, dancing and demonstrating. Jews in other countries watched with amazement as pride in being Jewish grew among a new generation of Russian Jews. Inspired by their willingness to "go public," Israeli and American Jews took to dancing outside on this holiday as well.

Jewish identity—over and above, despite, or simply apart from religion—has been a source of meaning for many Jews. For Jews in America, identity is often linked to Jewish vulnerability and survival, focusing on anti-Semitism. But a sense of connection to the Jewish people can also emerge through pride when individual Jews or Jewish groups act in ways that we admire. Jewish identity may be a significant bond for you as a couple. It may provide a shared interest that may lead you to travel, to the study of history, and to activism that enriches your lives. If only one of you is Jewish, it is important to be mindful of how powerful this pull can be for the Jewish partner—sometimes when least expected.

Evelyn and Norm hadn't belonged to a synagogue in five years. After their younger daughter's bat mitzvah, they left the temple, to which they had felt only minimally connected.

Although both of them comfortably and clearly identified as Jews, that meant very little on a day-to-day basis. One day a good friend invited them to go on a vacation to Argentina and introduced them to members of the struggling Jewish community there. Evelyn and Norm were so moved that upon their return they both became deeply involved in their local Jewish Federation's work on behalf of Argentine Jews.

You may find many ways—ritual, study, and reaching out—to incorporate your sense of connection with other Jews into your life as a couple.

Marking the Seasons of Our Lives

As we think about our days and years together as a couple, we realize there are moments in our lives that we may already formally acknowledge and others that we might consider marking. Simḥat Torah may help us consider some of these in a new way.

Nature, History, and Our Spiraling Lives

Simḥat Torah, like most Jewish holidays, draws our attention to the intersection of history and nature. The Torah reading includes the death of Moses, a signal event in the story of the Jewish people. When we roll the scroll back to the beginning, we are reading about the creation of the world, an event in the universal story of nature. Both the stories of the natural world and the history of a particular people are entwined in the holiday celebrations. Jewish holidays are often keyed to the cycles of nature: Ḥanukkah to the darkness of the winter solstice, Pesaḥ to the budding of hope in spring, Sukkot to the harvest of fall. Nature serves as a backdrop to the linear biblical narrative of the Jewish journey: slavery to freedom to covenant to the death of Moses, and on into the Promised Land. This linear view holds open the promise of getting it better the next time.

Your life together is both circular and linear. You may notice as the years go by how the seasons shape your experience of each other and your time together, and how certain themes recur in each season. The story of your relationship also moves forward in time. Each year is new and can be shaped to some extent by your choices. You might think of it as a spiral: Each time you cycle you have the potential to move forward or upward. You may feel as if you have the same argument year after year, but in reality, each year you have the possibility of doing it differently.

Boredom to Exultation

Lauren and Roger always had an active, busy life. Now they were going through a slow time. Roger had been laid off in the downsizing after the dot.com bust. The area where they lived offered few opportunities for employment. Between benefits from the old job, savings, and Lauren's income, the couple was stable financially, but life had become gray. Roger desperately missed working and the sense of identity it gave him. Lauren, busy at her job all week, noticed his boredom and listlessness on weekends, and found it contagious. Both of them realized that they needed to find a way to help Roger feel that he was making a contribution of some sort during this flat period. They looked for something they could share, something that would engage both of them physically and intellectually. They found they were interested in birds, and after joining in some weekend bird-watches, Roger began to organize bird-watching trips for others. This gave him a new focus for his weekday time and both of them an activity they enjoyed together on weekends.

Our lives as couples have a rhythm not unlike that of the festival year—that is to say, an uneven, ragged one. There can be a great deal of excitement concentrated in a few years, followed by stretches of arid time. Our months and years are not neatly balanced with happy and sad, demanding and easy, arranged in a sensible order. We rush to keep up, then stand still and wait. After a while, as a couple, we learn to use our imagination and creativity to redeem our time.

Simhat Torah was an afterthought. It emerged in Europe around the eleventh century to address a problem: There was a two-day biblical holiday called Shemini Atzeret tacked on to the end of Sukkot. The purpose of this holiday had been lost to the ages. So people had difficulty getting emotionally charged up for yet another two-day celebration, in the wake of a full month of holidays: Rosh Hashanah, Yom Kippur, and Sukkot.

The Rabbis noticed that the Torah reading for the second day of Shemini Atzeret was the last chapters of Deuteronomy, the last book of the Torah. Lest the devil think they were quitting (as they put it in the language of the time), they turned around and immediately read the first chapter of Genesis, the Torah reading for the upcoming Sabbath. They developed this ritual into the centerpiece of a new holiday that they called Simhat Torah.

This transition from end to beginning evolved into a glorious celebration of the cycle of the year itself, a dramatic opportunity to acknowledge the power of the Torah and of our ongoing engagement with it. Oftentimes, we need to bring this same creativity to the rhythms of our days and years. We can create holidays of our own. When we come to a place in our journey where we are just slogging through, we need to draw on all our powers to come up with something that will allow us to celebrate.

Mordecai Kaplan described the second day of all the festivals as "wiping yourself after a shower with a wet towel."

Anniversaries

One of the staples of the sitcom view of American marriage is the wife who anticipates flowers and treats on her wedding anniversary and the husband who forgets what day it is. Like many other rituals in our society, the wedding anniversary, at least for some couples, has become lifeless. The canned sentiments provided by Hallmark cards strive unsuccessfully to enliven it.

What are the anniversaries you share as a couple? The day you met? The day you realized you were going to try to spend your lives together? You might try celebrating your anniversaries, the ones that matter the most to you, in the spirit of Sim<u>h</u>at Torah. You have been through a year's cycle together, made it through all the seasons and whatever pleasure and pain the year has brought. You have fought; you have reconciled; you have exulted in professional triumphs; you have lost friends. You have wrestled with each story as it unfolded.

Now you are preparing to start another year of marriage, to enter the cycle again, despite and because of all that has happened. What can you do together to heighten the holiness of the endeavor, with all its disappointments, surprises, and wonder, and celebrate your loyalty to the process? The reading of the Torah from the creation of the world to the death of Moses includes the whole range of human emotions, just like a year in our lives. Some of the portions are exhilarating, and some we would rather skip—in the Torah cycle and in life.

Your "anniversary" celebration might be an evening of looking at old scrapbooks, slides, or videos, reviewing the year that has gone by. It might be the time to go out and buy yourselves something special or do something offbeat that you've been wanting to do. This might be a night to study together in <u>hevruta</u>—perhaps your wedding vows, your *ketubah*, or the Seven Blessings of the Jewish wedding service.

Consider taking your wedding rings off and putting them back on each other's fingers. This can be an annual ritual. However, since it is traditional to remove all rings before the ritual washing of hands on Shabbat eve, some couples make sure to replace each other's rings after the washing and thus reaffirm their vows fifty-two times a year.

The Space between the End and the Beginning

When something ends, we need to begin something else, and we need to notice the space in between. When the Torah scroll is completed with the reading of the end of Deuteronomy, it is promptly begun again with the first verses of Genesis—but it takes some time to roll the scroll back to the beginning (or to take out a second Torah scroll, already positioned at Genesis). Though the lag time is not great, it allows for a pause before we leap into the story again. As a couple you may be entering a new life stage, and you sense that while some doors are closing, others may be opening. You may even be in the moment of pause. Have you thought of creating a ritual to mark that time between the end and the beginning?

Harriet and Jill were on vacation when their home burned to the ground with everything they owned inside. The shared devastation was harrowing. They were called to begin again, but how?

Ellen discovered that Marvin was having an affair. At first it felt like the end of everything, but as the weeks passed, they both understood that they could be at the beginning of something new.

Barbara Kingsolver offers these words:

> In my own worst seasons I've come back from the colorless world of despair by forcing myself to look hard, for a long time, at a single glorious thing ... until I learned to be in love with my life again. Like a stroke victim retraining new parts of the brain to grasp lost skills, I have taught myself joy over and over again.

At Simhat Torah we celebrate the learning that comes in the space in between and the sheer guts and trust it often takes to start anew.

Closure

When we finally finish something, how do we mark that it is done? Upon completion of the study of a particular subject or book, students and teachers traditionally make a special party, or *siyum*. There is food and drink and celebration. The tradition even permits certain fasts to be overridden by the requirement to feast at a *siyum*. Simhat Torah is a mega-*siyum*.

We all have probably given a party after completing a major work project or for graduation from school. A *siyum* is more than just a celebration. At a *siyum*, the people who have completed their learning share some piece of what they learned with those who are gathered, and in closing they bless their teachers.

If you have experienced a major change during the year, such as the loss of a loved one, the wedding of a child, a move, or a job transition, you can mark the moment with a prayer. As the Torah scroll is rolled from Deuteronomy back to Genesis (or as you finish looking at the pictures from the year since your last anniversary), you can say, "Just as the Torah is rolled from place to place amid joy, so too may we roll from place to place surrounded by compassion." *K'shem shehaTorah niglelet mimakom l'-makom b'simhah uv'shalom, ken niglol mi-makom l'makom b'rahamim uv'ratzon.*

If you have been through a hard time as a couple, throw a *siyum* when it is over. It could be just for the two of you, or you might invite close friends. You have had the courage to make it through. Now take some time to talk about what you have learned in the process. Bless the sources of wisdom, whatever they might have been, that were your teachers. Perhaps you will want to use the traditional words Jews say when they complete the reading of a book of the Torah: _Hazak, hazak, v'nithazeik!_ Be strong, be strong and let us strengthen each other! Then celebrate in whatever mode lets your soul dance.

Celebrations/_Minhagim_

Create a ritual of commitment that would make your anniversary more meaningful.

Go dancing on or near Simhat Torah.

Arrange to take a dance class or pursue some other new hobby together that is active and fun.

Schedule a time, once a month, when you will go out together and move your bodies—in whatever ways you enjoy.

Agree to meet once a week for an hour and read your favorite book aloud to each other.

Take turns teaching each other something one of you knows and the other does not, and bless each other for teaching.

Agree to learn something new together.

• Host a _siyum_ just for each other, or for friends, when you have completed the learning.

Learn calligraphy (Hebrew or English) and copy a favorite quotation to frame and hang in your home.

Join a book group (Jewish or general) together.

Use wine (or honey) from Israel for your holiday celebration.

Take a class together in Hebrew, Yiddish, Jewish music, Jewish history, or any subject that appeals to you.

Learning with a Partner/<u>H</u>evruta

These are the obligations without measure: leaving crops at the corner of a field for the poor, offering first fruits as a gift to the Temple, bringing special offerings to the Temple on the three festivals, doing deeds of loving-kindness, and studying Torah. These are the obligations that yield immediate fruit and continue to yield fruit in time to come: honoring parents, doing deeds of loving-kindness, attending the house of study daily, welcoming the stranger, visiting the sick, rejoicing with bride and groom, consoling the bereaved, praying with sincerity, making peace when there is strife. And the study of Torah is equal to them all.

—**Mishnah Peah** 1:1

Questions for Discussion

1. Do you agree that study and good deeds are equal?

2. If not, how would you describe their relationship?

3. How do you balance study and action in your own lives?

4. What do you think of this list of activities?

5. How well is each of you doing with these commandments from the Torah?

6. What would you put on your own list of important activities?

7. How do you help each other do these activities, or the ones on your own list, in your daily lives?

8. Is there one particular activity you are both eager to make more prominent in your life together?

The way of Torah requires forty-eight qualifications:
Learning, attention, clarity of mind and tongue,
An intuitive heart, awe, reverence, humility, joy,
Simplicity, apprenticeship to sages,
Friendship with colleagues, challenging students,
Calm deliberation,
Knowledge of Scripture and Mishnah,
Balance in business, worldly affairs,
And sexual intimacy,
Sufficient sleep,
Avoiding gossip, maintaining humor,
Slow to anger, with a gentle heart,
Trusting the sages, accepting suffering,
Knowing one's calling, rejoicing in one's portion,
Guarding one's words,
Not claiming merit for oneself,
Being loved,
Loving God, humanity, charity and reproof,
Not seeking out honors,
Not boasting of one's education,
Being loath to judge,
Sharing the burdens of others,
Giving people the benefit of the doubt,
Leading others to truth and peace,
Being meticulous in study,
Asking probing questions,
Answering queries honestly,
Listening and discussing,
Learning in order to teach and practice,
Honoring one's teacher's wisdom with questions,

Contemplation,
Giving credit to those who taught one—
Whoever credits a teaching to its author
Brings redemption to the world.

—Rami Shapiro, based on *Pirkei Avot* 6:6

Ways to Use This Text

Study this passage with your partner, taking one qualification a day for forty-eight days.

Discuss the meaning of the qualification and how it applies to each of your lives.

"The best thing for being sad," replied Merlin, beginning to puff and blow, "is to learn something. That's the only thing that never fails. You may grow old and trembling in your anatomies, you may lie awake at night listening to the disorder of your veins ... There is only one thing for it then—to learn. Learn why the world wags and what wags it. That is the only thing which the mind can never exhaust, never alienate, never be tortured by, never fear or distrust, and never dream of regretting. Learning is the only thing for you. Look what a lot of things there are to learn."

—T. H. White

Questions for Discussion

1. When has each of you been in need of renewal?

2. What role does learning play in your emotional lives?

3. What are some times when learning has been spiritual for you?

4. Are there things you would like to learn together now?

5. How would you teach yourselves joy?

Reaching Out/*Gemilut* <u>H</u>esed

Get involved in literacy training.

Collect books and donate them to needy people or programs.

Volunteer in a tutoring or mentoring program, perhaps at your synagogue.

- If none exists, consider creating one.

- Some synagogues match young children with adults in the community who can help them with their homework.

- Bar and bat mitzvah–age children may need help with writing their speeches or learning a new skill, or they may just appreciate a grown-up who is not their parent taking a sincere interest in their Jewish studies.

Contribute money to the purchase of a Torah for your congregation or another congregation that needs one, or to the local library or an after-school tutoring program.

Write a letter to a teacher you have known, perhaps many years ago. Say how much his or her teaching has meant to you.

- If possible, bring your partner to meet this teacher.

Celebrate an anniversary by giving back some gift to the world. For example, on the anniversary of your children's births you might want to go together to donate blood.

Contribute to the American Jewish World Service (AJWS) to support its outreach to Jews and others in developing countries around the world.

Consider joining an AJWS delegation to one of the communities in which the organization is funding grassroots, sustainable development. See www.ajws.org.

Shabbat

Shabbat (the Sabbath) begins at sunset each Friday and continues through sunset on Saturday. According to the Bible, God created the world in six days; on the seventh day "God ceased/rested (*yishbot*) from all the work that God had done, and God blessed the seventh day and declared it holy" (Genesis 2:2–3). Since biblical times, Jews have attempted to follow this pattern of work and rest: six days engaged in the world, one day devoted to the soul.

This holy day of blessing and renewal, sometimes personified as a bride or a queen, is made distinctive by a complex weave of traditional laws and customs. These include a multitude of prohibitions against "work"—defined in various and evolving ways. They also include positive commandments, such as eating festive meals on Friday night and Saturday, lighting and blessing candles, sanctifying the day over a cup of wine, and blessing and eating a ḥallah, a braided, sweetened egg bread. Saturday morning is traditionally devoted to communal worship and reading of the weekly Torah portion. As darkness falls on Saturday evening, *Havdalah*, a plaintive ceremony of Separation, usually performed at home, marks the reluctant farewell to the Sabbath for another week.

CHAPTER NINE

Pausing to Bless What Is:
Shabbat

Will

Three generations back
my family had only

to light a candle
and the world parted.

Today, Friday afternoon,
I disconnect clocks and phones.

When night fills my house
with passages,

I begin saving
my life.

—Marcia Falk, from The Book of Blessings

There are no lists at the end of this chapter—no rituals to practice, no documents to study, no acts of loving-kindness to perform. Shabbat is filled with rituals, it is often a wonderful time for partners to study together, and there are ways to reach out to the world that are uniquely suited to the day. Yet this discussion of Shabbat stands alone, without assignments, suggestions, or "to-dos." The reason is simple: Shabbat is not about doing. It is not about adding anything but noticing and blessing what is already here. Each holiday has its own perspective on remembering the past. Shabbat, on the other hand, is about being present. You have been through the yearly cycle of work and of joy; you have learned and grown as individuals and as a couple. This chapter is about saying, as God did at the end of the sixth day, "Behold, it is very good" (Genesis 1:31).

A Time to Bless

Roz used to commute daily between her office in North Philadelphia and her home in a far suburb of the city. Her route involved changing trains at a particularly gritty station. This meant standing on a platform for about seven minutes each afternoon with a crowd of strangers waiting for the second train to arrive. One Friday, one of the men on the platform turned to her and said, "TGIF! Thank God it's Friday."

Another said, "You know, we stand here every day together waiting for the 5:45, and we don't even know each other's names."

A third said, "Next Friday, I'll bring a bottle of wine."

"I'll bring cups."

"I'll bring chips."

The following week this merry group of commuters had their first TGIF party. It lasted exactly seven minutes. Then they all got on the second train and went home for the weekend. The custom lasted for years. The celebrants changed over time, but the constant was the victory they shared rescuing a little swatch of gray, urban life and turning it into a party.

TGIF: Thank God it's Friday. Western civilization has made this idea part of its world. Even though the Sabbath in America has devolved into the weekend, longer and much different, it still resembles its ancestor enough so that people get the idea. TGIF!

The concept behind Shabbat is as simple as the bumper sticker version: *Even God took a vacation.* In the biblical story, God created each of the elements of the world in six days and rested on the seventh. But the seventh was not merely a throwaway. Creation took seven days; on the seventh day God created rest.

Shabbat is the day we stop worrying about what should be and look with appreciation at what is, the day we stop trying to do, and revel in simply being. For couples, the idea means that we need to pause sometime during every week, perhaps even every day, and simply bless what is.

Blessing What Is

We have more timesaving devices than ever before, yet we seem to be always running out of time. How much of our lives are we missing in our rush to get on to the next thing? "Dayeinu," the traditional song from the Pesah seder, is about stopping to bless what is. *Dayeinu* is Hebrew for "It would have been enough for us." The song goes through all the wondrous acts of liberation we celebrate at the seder, in the order in which they happened. After mentioning each one, the rousing chorus proclaims "Dayeinu—that alone would have been enough!" What do we mean when we say, "It would have been enough"? Wasn't each step of the journey necessary? If the sea had split, but we had not survived in the wilderness, it would *not* have been enough.

Dayeinu is about seeing the world from the perspective of Shabbat. If we imagine the Israelites at each stage of their journey to freedom, we can picture them reacting in different ways. In one image they are anxious: "OK, we got through the Red

Sea today, but what is going to happen tomorrow?" This is not an inappropriate thought and is probably worth thinking, six days a week. In another image, the Shabbat version, they simply pause and say, "Even if nothing else happens for us, this is truly worthy of blessing and thanks. Dayeinu!"

Take a few minutes right now to think about what you cherish in your partner. Be sure not to keep it to yourself. Share it with your partner. Dayeinu.

Grace and Gratitude

Shabbat begins Friday night with a festive meal. Hallah is the bread of choice for Jews who follow European traditions. Whatever bread is served, it is customary to offer two loaves of bread with the dinner. The pair of loaves reminds us of manna, the miraculous food God is said to have provided for the Israelites in the wilderness. Manna was grace—it simply fell from the sky in just the amounts needed. The Torah reports that on the day before Shabbat, a double portion of manna was provided (Exodus 16:23). When we see the two loaves on the table, we can recall that gift of sustenance and all the gifts of our lives.

Shabbat is a time to hone our gratitude for each other. It is traditional for a husband to bless his wife on Friday night and for both parents to bless their children. Janice and her husband had never felt comfortable with the blessing of the wife, but they always blessed their children. When the children left home, the parents looked at each other and wondered, "What now?" Having adopted an Atkins diet, they had neither bread nor wine on the table. They laughed, lit the candles and, awkwardly, tentatively, using words of their own making, began to figure out how to bless each other.

Friday night dinner in the Sabbath tradition is a feast. It can be an invitation for a couple to seek out and create more feasts in their lives. Feasts may involve food, but they don't have to. A feast can be anything that nourishes us, anything that we enjoy with intentionality and for which we express gratitude. We can have a feast as long as we feel fully indulged and suitably grateful for our windfall. For you it may be two loaves of ḥallah on Friday night or spending the night listening to every CD ever made by your favorite musician, no matter how long it takes. Whatever it is, try to be fully present for the festivity.

Why do we have to make a special effort to notice what is good and to express gratitude for it? Studies have shown that we recall happy memories in a kind of haze but remember distinctly the painful details of terrible times. Scientists hypothesize that as our species developed, it was to our survival advantage to take clear note of things that went wrong so that we would avoid them in the future. Yet for our spiritual well-being, it is best to be able to savor and cherish the good. Jewish tradition includes a commandment about "noticing the good" (*hakarat hatov*). Saying a blessing or offering words of gratitude allows us to keep the good in our minds so it can continue to nourish us.

Rules That Liberate

For those who live in traditional Jewish communities, Shabbat is the scaffolding of their week, but for some Jews it is hard to know where to begin. For many, a discussion of Shabbat immediately raises the issue of what is allowed and what is forbidden. Shabbat seems to be about rules: rules broken; rules forgotten; rules never fully understood. Jews and those who live with them ask, "What is it exactly you are supposed to do or not do on this day?" Sometimes those asking the questions feel guilty, sometimes annoyed, sometimes curious, and often just plain confused.

The rules serve some people well. When they were first married, William and Manny were graduate students in different fields, studying and working every day of the week. After a few months, they noticed that they were creating busy parallel lives. They wanted to ensure that their lives would intersect in meaningful ways. William, who was not born Jewish, had studied Judaism with a rabbi before their wedding. He suggested that they take a look at the traditional rules of Shabbat and carefully sift through them to find the ones that made sense to them. They liked the idea of not using a car; not driving would mean staying close to home. Each week they looked forward to their day of restrictions, their day of being together. It was, paradoxically, their day of freedom. They often wondered, as the years passed, how their relationship could have thrived without it.

Other people discover Shabbat late in life. Jules, a professor at an Ivy League university, had been going to synagogues on and off for many, many decades. No matter what the sermons he heard said, he always understood the rules about not working on Shabbat as this: Either you observed them or you did not. He, like most people he knew, did not. When he officially retired, in his mid-seventies, Jules found he was still researching and writing. Both he and his wife wanted him to slow down, but nothing seemed to help him do that. Finally someone suggested that he simply give up work one day a week—it did not matter which—as a kind of "Shabbat." He decided to experiment with not working on Saturday for a few weeks. As the weeks stretched into months, he discovered new activities and pleasures, and his relationship with his wife improved as well. Finally, Jules was able to relax the more rigid constraints and still preserve the joy he had discovered in binding himself to a day of freedom.

Setting Aside Sacred Time

When you thought about the Maccabees who ritually purified their Temple and rededicated it at Hanukkah, you considered how you handle your own shared space so that it serves your life together. Time, too, needs to be consecrated. As a culture, we have become entirely too busy. Sometimes it is our schedules that require treatment.

Karla and Becky were so caught up in their careers and their high-powered lives that they joked they would have to learn "speed relaxing." As they drifted increasingly out of touch with each other, problems that should have surfaced went underground. Eventually they sought the help of a marriage therapist. Week after week, Tuesdays at noon became the sacred time in their lives when they abandoned the computer, turned off their cell phones, and sat quietly with each other for an hour—talking, reflecting, being. The therapist offered some insights, but some of the best learning for Karla and Becky was simply that they needed to guard time for each other.

If you have had children, you have probably noticed that "quality time" does not always work as you hoped. You need to put in many, many hours with young children. The investment of time in sufficient quantity will yield some percentage of quality—but it may be when you least expect it and on *their* schedule. As adults, however, we can train ourselves to make good use of a scarce resource. When we set aside time, particularly if it is at regular and habitual intervals (as in the traditional Sabbath), we can learn to use that time exceptionally well.

Some couples find that they can adapt the concept of Shabbat to their daily routine. They plan for a certain time each day to turn off the computer and be with one another (or their children) in soul-satisfying ways. Lenny and Rena have tea at the kitchen table every night at eleven. They sit together for a half-hour, talk over the day, and appreciate each other. They do it each night, even when they are tired or stressed, because they know that is when they need it most.

Taking a Break

Marcy and Stan routinely started the weekend with the same argument. Marcy wanted to go to the gym alone on Saturday morning, then get some shopping done and meet a friend for coffee. Stan wanted the two of them to be together the whole day. Actually, they were both eager to avoid too much intimacy, but they went about keeping their distance in very different ways. Stan finally began to realize this, and that he was ready for more closeness. After reading a book about Judaism, he decided to try out the idea of Shabbat. His first thought, to engage Marcy in home-based rituals and activities, was an obvious nonstarter. Then he realized that to truly observe Shabbat, he needed to stop "doing." For him that meant accepting the degree of closeness or distance Marcy wanted. In choosing to yield peacefully to her rhythm for those twenty-four hours, Stan broke the cycle that had kept them apart. At first Marcy was shocked by her new freedom to come and go as she pleased. But as she began to relax, they were able to find a quiet open space in which to gradually enjoy each other again. A kind of Shabbat, quite different from the traditional one, emerged in their lives.

Some couples find it good to just take a break from arguments altogether. The traditional greeting "Shabbat Shalom" ("Sabbath peace") reminds us that this day is a good one to recall the value placed on peace. Ritual practice, old and new, reinforces this notion.

Jenny and Sam always made sure not to use a knife to cut the ḥallah on Shabbat because knives are instruments of war. As they tore the ḥallah with their hands, they also thought about what it could mean in their own lives to refrain from conflict for a day. Many things had to be discussed and even argued about during the week. But one day off, one day devoted to peacefulness in their little corner of the world, was a good goal to strive for.

Sex and Shabbat

Marriage counselors are famous for prescribing dates with your partner, particularly ones with sensual props. The same romantic cues appear over and over in the books about renewing your relationship: candles, luxurious food, wine, flowers, baths, or Jacuzzis.

Is it just a coincidence that the basics of the romantic date track so closely the symbols of Shabbat: candles, special bread and other good food, wine, and, traditionally, immersion in a ritual bath? Traditionally, Jewish men went to the ritual bath before Shabbat. Jewish tradition has understood the eve of Shabbat to be a particularly auspicious night for married couples to be intimate. The Talmud includes the injunction that "A Torah scholar should take care to fulfill conjugal duties to his spouse on the eve of the Sabbath" (*Ketubot* 62b). In an eighteenth-century prayer book by Rabbi Jacob Emden, the laws governing sexual relations for a married couple are printed in the section just following the Friday night home prayers. Sex on Shabbat with one's marital partner is considered, according to the folk saying, to be a "double mitzvah" (commandment), combining the holiness of conjugal relations with the holiness of Shabbat.

Since many of us do not consider ourselves bound by commandments in the first place, what can we take from all this for our own lives? Other mammals seem to engage in sexual encounters without nearly the fuss and

After her children began attending a Jewish preschool, Gwen became increasingly interested in every aspect of Judaism. Her husband was resolute in his lack of involvement. The one and only aspect of her new commitment for which he showed the slightest enthusiasm was the "double mitzvah on Shabbat." As Gwen put it, "It's a start."

emotional turmoil we humans bring to them. One thing is certain: When things are not going well with a couple, problems are often played out in their interactions around sexual relations. Can thinking about the connection between Shabbat and sex help us move past some of the complications we create and keep our focus on what is important?

The tradition of having sex on Shabbat eve provides a fixed, scheduled sexual encounter. Such a schedule can be restorative. Couples who are having conflict or stress around their sexual relationship are often wise to "make a date," quite apart from any idea of Shabbat. The date takes the pressure and anxiety off the nondate times and helps them to find a rhythm that separates their lovemaking from their power struggles.

But Shabbat adds a deeper dimension. While the creation of the next generation is an important value in Jewish tradition, privileging Shabbat as a time for sexual intimacy has no impact at all on the likelihood of conceiving a child. This makes it clear that sexual relations are valued in their own right and that they are connected to spiritual aims.

The *Zohar*, a classic text of Jewish mysticism, teaches that when a husband and wife unite in body, "The Divine Presence establishes itself." What does this mean? For each of us, there are ways that sexual intimacy relates to our deeper longings for spiritual intimacy and becomes part of our connection to what we consider divine.

Both scheduling and the spiritual dimension were factors in the issues that confronted Lili and George. Like many couples who struggle for years with infertility, they had almost resigned themselves to sex becoming a duty and a chore. Their high-priced fertility specialist rigidly scheduled their sexual encounters, and the whole enterprise was now tied up in their minds with stress and failure. It was hard to know when to have relations aside from the assigned times or even to remember why they would want to. When they agreed to have sex on Friday nights, completely separate from their fertility regime, they reclaimed this part of their relationship for goals unrelated to procreation. Knowing that Jewish tradition had long understood this time in the week as a holy one, they were able to approach Friday night bedtime encounters in a very different spirit.

For some couples, it is not procreation but rather sexual fulfillment that becomes an all-consuming goal, making their encounters in bed charged with goal-directed anxiety. The titles of recent books on the subject (*Orgasms for Two, The Big Bang, The Good Vibrations*) reflect our culture's transformation of lovemaking into sport. The idea that the act of love is connected to the holiness of the Sabbath may help couples focus on something deeper and more meaningful than technique. Friday nights can be a time to just enjoy each other without any thought of performance.

What are the times and places that would link lovemaking with holiness for you? What are the visual and sensual props that would enhance your sense of the multiple levels of connection in the act of making love? Perhaps your notion of God is tied deeply to nature, and you have found that some of your most memorable lovemaking has been out-of-doors. You and your partner might want to think of how you can bring that into your routine lives, much as the Shabbat rituals bring the Divine Presence into the home. Perhaps you might want to build a skylight over your bed or play a tape recording of nature sounds or decorate your bedroom with natural treasures or photographs. And candles are almost always a good addition.

Refocusing

Even in the midst of a big city, Shabbat turns our attention to the sky. While most everything in our highly advanced civilization runs according to the clock, Shabbat still is keyed to nature's cycles. If we follow tradition, we light Shabbat candles eighteen minutes before sunset, and we end Shabbat with *Havdalah* Saturday night after the appearance of three stars. These times vary through the year, and while we can look them up in a Jewish calendar or almanac, we can also simply look outside—an activity that can help attune us to the interplay of light and darkness. The times for Shabbat differ with the seasons, and so we notice the year as it cycles through its changes.

Consider what it might mean to get in touch with the natural cycles of the days and nights. That connection can remind us of our own origins as creatures of this earth. Before we were such complicated, civilized beings, masters of our environment, we had to pay attention to nature. Couples often notice how different life is when, by choice or necessity, they find themselves without electricity for a time. They huddle together around the light they create in a fireplace or with candles. They enjoy this brief interlude. And what is it about Niagara Falls that makes that spot a honeymoon destination? There is something about the world-as-given, before humans have a chance to decorate or alter it, that brings us back to a simpler state of mind. Paying attention to that world teaches us awe, humility, and a sense of being part of a vast creation with its own rhythms.

You might want to think about the experiences you and your partner have shared that help you to bring that spirit to your interactions. Perhaps you love to backpack through the mountains to remind yourselves that "things take time." Perhaps you enjoy gardening on the rooftop of your urban apartment and eating the vegetables in season. Maybe you slow down by collecting sunsets or sunrises together (you have to sit quietly while they unfold). Or perhaps you share your home with an animal, a creature that lives close to the ground, never far from the basics of this earthly existence.

How have you been nurtured by your connections to nature? Do you want to be more creative in how you relate in the future? Some couples build waterfalls in their backyard or place a miniature fountain on a table in their living room and spend time together contemplating them and soaking up the negative ions that are said to create positive energy. Others like to lie on their backs and look at the moon and the stars. The ebb and flow of the ocean can calm us as we consider the fluctuations in our own lives. Take a walk together and think it over.

Getting and Spending

According to Jewish law, one must not handle money during Shabbat. It became a tradition that the last money to leave someone's pocket before Shabbat was dedicated to *tzedakah*, righteous giving. Some families keep their *tzedakah* boxes right next to their Shabbat candles. These boxes can be simple tin cans, provided by a Jewish charity you support, or beautiful works of art.

In the days when the Christian Sabbath was enforced in America, Sunday, like the Jewish Sabbath, was a time when commerce was forbidden, and in some states there are still vestiges of this. But for the most part, modern commercial society has overtaken the idea of a day without cash. Even Christian bookstores are often open on Sundays. While America rapidly loses this tradition of a shopping-free day, the issue of money continues to loom large for many couples: how much to spend, how much to save, how much they have.

Maggie and Ed fought about money. They knew it was because there was never as much as either would have liked, and they had different visions of how to spend what felt like a scarce resource. They went to a wise rabbi who gave them what seemed like bizarre advice. She counseled them to start giving more *tzedakah* each week just before Shabbat. Give away more money just when it feels most scarce? At first they thought she was joking, but Maggie and Ed were so anxious and unhappy that they decided to give it a try. Strangely, as soon as they began this routine, they started to feel richer. Giving money away to those who needed it more than they did helped them to regain perspective on the place of money in their lives. Most important, the couple was able to reconnect with each other. They shared a fundamental value of justice and charity, and in giving *tzedakah* they remembered the ideals that had brought them together.

The idea of having a day when we don't spend money can make us mindful of the power money has over us. Shabbat is a day when people traditionally stopped spending and getting, and contented themselves with what they already had. It can be a day to think about what we don't need to buy. For all of us it can be an opportunity to focus on what is really important. There is something powerful in insulating one-seventh of life from the consumerist culture. As our society becomes ever more materialistic, this antidote grows in importance.

Dale and Hank came from very different religious traditions. As a couple they have sought community in other ways. Because they had chosen to be childless, they had many opportunities to travel. Early in their relationship, they realized that it was not important to them to see yet another Club Med on their summer vacation. They seek out meaningful, service-oriented experiences instead. They have traveled with interfaith groups for two weeks at a time each summer, working in an orphanage in Haiti and helping to build a community center in El Salvador, among other activities. They have returned from each trip aware of the plentitude with which they are blessed. They feel like this time off from consumer culture gives them something invaluable and connects them to each other in an important way. Like Shabbat, the break returns them to their lives with heightened awareness and gratitude.

Planning and Serendipity

A folktale tells of a group of Jews who decided to see if they could "make *Shabbes*" on Wednesday. Sure enough, once they did all the proper preparations, the Shabbat Queen thought it was Friday night and descended! As we have seen, we have to "make" the Sabbath, just like we have to make all the holidays. Some people plan ahead throughout the week to "make *Shabbes*." If a new seasonal fruit or vegetable appears in the market on Tuesday, they buy it but save it to be served at Shabbat dinner. If they acquire a new item of clothing, they wait till Shabbat to wear it for the first time. They think about ways to make that day special, with fresh flowers, new sheets, or a good wine.

Each of us finds our own ways to "make *Shabbes*," to create time devoted to renewal. In the villages of Eastern Europe, where Jews often worked with their hands, they would clean up and put on their best garments to greet the Shabbat Queen. They felt like royalty, privileged to spend a day indoors, praying and studying. Today, when some of us work all week with books, dressed in suits and good shoes, Shabbat may mean changing into our favorite jeans and comfortable work shirt, eating a good meal, and digging in the garden for a few hours. We must be purposeful in our efforts.

But all our work is only part of the story. Another folktale tells of a rabbi who entertained a Roman emperor on Shabbat. The emperor was so impressed with the wonderful food he was served that he insisted on getting detailed recipes to pass on to his servants. When the servants prepared the food according to specification, the results were disappointing. The emperor insisted on knowing what had gone wrong. In one version of the story, the rabbi explains to the emperor that he is missing the special spice. "I will buy the spice!" the emperor cries. But of course, the spice cannot be purchased, even by an emperor, for the special spice is Shabbat itself (*Shabbat* 119a).

In a marriage there is also a spice that cannot be purchased. Observing Shabbat in some form, wonderful as it may be, will not necessarily create it. No one can write you the recipe for it. There is always some mystery about the way the spice that can't be named enters, leaves, and emerges again in a relationship. This is the flip side of the notion that we can "make love." The spice that lifts something from edible to truly sublime remains elusive.

When they were first married, Louise and Sandy cherished their "we." To honor it was their highest priority, and they did it without effort. Then a series of stressful events—problems with aging parents and developing children—wore them down. Each retreated into her own "I" and found they were often fighting over who got her way. One summer, although the problems had far from vanished, they were both enjoying a sailing vacation when Louise asked Sandy, "You seem to be happy on this boat. Are you really having fun or are you just happy because you know how much I love sailing?" Sandy was surprised to realize she could not answer that question. Her personal happiness was not something separate from her partner's happiness. This was not a matter of "goodwill" or "sacrifice" on her part. She said a silent prayer of thanks. Quietly, without her noticing it, the "we" had returned.

We cannot ever fully understand that mystery. Once again, we return to the duality of control and surrender. We may plan to create the conditions for that special something to emerge in a hundred ways, big and small. We work on our relationships. We "make *Shabbes*," and we make love. At the same time, there is that which is beyond our control, serendipity. We can think of it like the Shabbat spice, and we can, even as we work and strive, notice its coming and going with a nod of appreciation to the Unknown.

Taking our Leave

Like all the holidays, Shabbat comes to an end. At *Havdalah*, we separate from the holy day and turn our attention to the work ahead. We express our hope that we can hold a little bit of Shabbat inside us through the week. Jewish communities around the world have different traditions for "holding on to the blessing." Moroccan Jews, for example, dab a bit of the *Havdalah* wine on the napes of their necks and put a drop in each pocket for good luck in the coming week. We sniff sweet spices, a final whiff of the lingering sweetness of this time out of time.

Finally, we light a braided candle, for a simple one will not do. Through the holiday cycle we have seen that life is a complex weave of light and darkness, bitter and sweet, striving and surrendering. The twisted candle reminds us that as a couple our two lives have become entwined as one. Two souls enter a partnership, interwoven yet always distinct, joined by a third strand, the Divine Presence. As we perform the ritual of *Havdalah*, we hold our hands up to the flame and catch the reflection of the last light on our fingertips. Then, in the words of Marge Piercy, "We drown the candle in the little lake of wine." We pray that the light will continue to shine through our words and deeds, in our homes and in the world.

Afterword

*I can only answer the question "What am I to do?"
if I can answer the prior question, "Of what story or
stories do I find myself a part?"*

—**Alasdair MacIntyre**

We began our journey through the year at Hanukkah with a discussion of stories—the tales we spin about who we are as individuals and as couples over time. Keeping the focus on ourselves
and our satisfactions, however, is likely to lead to disappointment.
Our personal stories need not be suspended in midair; they can
unfold within a greater universe of values and meanings. Rather
than seeing Judaism as a source of general principles or abstract
truths, our approach was to plunge into the celebration of the
holidays, placing our particular narratives in the context of larger
narratives, stories of the Jewish people and their stormy but loving long-term relationship with one another and with God.

Why look for stories larger than our own? As we talked to
couples at various stages of life, we heard the profound longing,
at every stage, for more closeness and love, for a chance—perhaps
the best one we have—to overcome the loneliness of existence.
At the same time, we heard the genuine fear that underlies these
efforts. As Cheryl put it, "You are telling me that at sixty, I should
work on my marriage? Sure. I could work really hard, find more
depth and commitment in my relationship with Mark, and what
would be the reward? He might die." Then, after thinking for a

few minutes, she added, "He surely will die.... It's scary to be so vulnerable. Sometimes it feels safer not to care too much."

Cheryl put her finger on the deepest source of our resistance to intimacy. The spiritual perspective we have offered in this guide does not resolve that issue. It does suggest, however, that we can take a bit more of a risk. Knowing that we are part of something greater enriches our days. The stories of the Jewish people remind us that there is a cycle of sorrow and joy that commenced well before our lives began and will continue when ours are long completed. The story of a created world that God saw was "good" and that will one day be made whole again sets our life story in a context. The meaning we intuit in that grand narrative gives meaning to our little stories as well, even if we cannot always see the connection.

When we stop our lives and say, "Behold, it is good," we are reenacting the cosmic narrative of God who, in the biblical story, also took a deep breath and called that rest and appreciation a part of creation. So we can gamble with our hearts and know that our stories and the stories of those we love *will* in fact end, but also know that the stories we lived within and through will continue.

We have made connections to tradition, to community, to the work of healing our world, and we know that these too will continue. We have learned new ways to remember the past and also to deeply treasure the moment. Even though the joy and connection we may achieve with another human on this earth is limited, there are moments when we can freeze time, hold it up to the light, and bless it. And if we do that often, we know we will have the faith to move, in hope, into unknown futures together. Partnering is still a risky venture. May it also be, for all of us, a richly rewarding one.

Notes

Introduction (pp. 1–13)

Morning prayer service: There are many versions of the prayer book published by the various movements in Judaism. For a complete, traditional prayer book, see Philip Birnbaum, *The Daily Prayerbook* (New York: Hebrew Publishing Company, 1977).

The world stands on three things: ritual, learning, and acts of loving-kindness (*Mishnah Avot* 1:2): Throughout this book, citations from the Mishnah will appear in the text immediately after the quotation. *Avot* refers to the section of the Mishnah; 1:2 are the chapter and verse. A good translation of the Mishnah is Herbert Danby, *The Mishnah* (New York: Oxford University Press, 1985).

Palaces in time: Heschel's book, *The Sabbath: Its Meaning for Modern Man,* is a great place to begin a study of the Jewish holidays. (See Suggestions for Further Reading.)

Special days as "inns": Michael Strassfeld's book *The Jewish Holidays* is an excellent resource for a more in-depth study of the year cycle. The quote we use is from page 1. (See Suggestions for Further Reading.)

I don't know exactly what a prayer is: From Mary Oliver, "The Summer Day," *House of Light* (Boston: Beacon, 1992).

The Hebrew word for ritual is minhag: For an introduction to the role of *minhagim* in Jewish life, see Scott-Martin Kosofsky, *The Book of Customs: A Complete Handbook for the Jewish Year* (Inspired by the *Yiddish Minhagimbukh,* Venice, 1593) (San Francisco: HarperCollins, 2004). For contemporary rituals, see the ever-growing collection at www. Ritualwell.org.

I set my table with metaphor: Linda Pastan, "Passover," *PM/AM: New and Selected Poems* (New York: Norton, 1982).

Berakhot 58a: Talmud, literally "study, instruction," refers to collections of Jewish laws, containing teachings, commentaries, discussions, and decisions of many generations of Rabbis. Throughout this book, citations from the Talmud will appear in the text immediately after the quotation. The Talmud always refers to the Babylonian Talmud, the longer and more frequently cited of the two Talmuds. *Berakhot* refers to the tractate; 58 is the page number; and *a* is the side of the page. There are several English translations of the Talmud available. The most accessible is the translation by Adin Steinsaltz, published by Random House. Unfortunately, not every tractate is available. For tractates not yet translated by Steinsaltz, see the Artscroll Series published by Mesorah Publications (different tractates are published in different years).

Conservation of spiritual energy: Mordecai Kaplan, *Judaism as a Civilization* (Philadelphia: Jewish Publication Society, 1994), p. 388.

May your study be passionate: From Danny Siegel, "A Blessing," in *Between Dust and Dance* (Spring Valley, NY: Town House Press, 1978).

We are here to do: From Rami Shapiro, *Wisdom of the Jewish Sages: A Modern Reading of Pirkei Avot* (New York: Harmony/Bell Tower, 1995).

As Rabbi Israel Salanter expressed it: For more information about Israel Salanter and the *Mussar* movement that he created, see Alan Morinis, *Climbing Jacob's Ladder: One Man's Journey to Rediscover a Jewish Spiritual Tradition* (New York: Random House, 2002). You can also learn more by visiting www.alanmorinis.com.

Commentators have suggested: For a discussion of this issue, see Joshua Gutoff, "Blessings and Ethics: The Spiritual Life of Justice," *Conservative Judaism,* 49, no. 4 (Summer 1997): 50–58.

A new learning is about to be born: Quoted by Nahum Glatzer, in *Franz Rosenzweig: His Life and Thought* (New York: Schocken Books, 1998), p. 231 (adapted).

What Samuel Dresner wrote: The Sabbath (New York: Burning Bush Press, 1970), p. 21.

Chapter 1 (pp. 14–31)

I have walked through many lives: From Stanley Kunitz, "The Layers," in *The Collected Poems of Stanley Kunitz* (New York: W. W. Norton and Co., 2002).

Ascribing new meanings to past events: For more about narrative psychology, see Daniel Taylor, *The Healing Power of Stories: Creating Yourself through the Stories of Your Life* (New York: Doubleday, 1996).

For Mike, who had been raised Methodist: For a detailed discussion of interfaith couples and the December holidays, read Judy Petsonk and Jim Remsen, *The Intermarriage Handbook: A Guide for Jews and Christians* (San Francisco: HarperCollins, 1990).

Hanukkat HaBayit: For more information about this ceremony, see *On the Doorposts of Your House* (New York: Central Conference of American Rabbis, 1994), p. 138ff.

Recalling a medieval Jewish practice for scaring away demons: For this and other superstitious practices in the Jewish tradition, see Joshua Trachtenberg, *Jewish Magic and Superstition: A Study of Folk Religion* (New York: Atheneum, 1987). Rabbi Rayzel Raphael of Philadelphia created the home rededication ritual described in this chapter.

Hanging a mezuzah: The *Shulkhan Aruckh, Yoreh Deah* 289:6 and its commentaries contain additional discussions about how to hang a mezuzah.

Pauline Wengeroff: Her memoir includes reports of many practices like this. See Henny Wenkart, *Rememberings: The World of a Russian-Jewish Woman in the Nineteenth Century* (Baltimore: University Press of Maryland, 2000).

For every human being there rises a light: Attributed to the Baal Shem Tov, quoted in Meyer Levin, *Classic Hassidic Tales* (New York: Dorset Press, 1959).

Once the realization: From Rainier Maria Rilke, "Solitude," in *Why We Stay Together: Twenty Writers on Marriage and Its Rewards*, ed. Jennifer Schwamm Willis (Berkeley, Calif.: Avalon Publishing Group, 2002).

This house displays our virtue: From Marge Piercy, "Housekeeping," in *My Mother's Body* (New York: Alfred A. Knopf, 1991).

Chapter 2 (pp. 32–49)

Our sincerest laughter: Percy Bysshe Shelly, "The Skylark," M. H. Abrams, ed., *The Norton Anthology of English Literature*, Volume 2 (New York: Norton, 2003).

Real laughter is: For a neurobiologist's perspective on laughter, see Robert Provine, *Laughter: A Scientific Investigation* (New York: Penguin Books, 2001).

I am what I am: Song title and lyric from the musical *La Cage Aux Folles,* Jerry Herman, 1983.

Seventy faces: This description is used to underscore the complex nature of Torah. It first appeared in the midrashic collection *Numbers Rabbah, Naso* 13:15.

When Rabbi Eleazar of Kosnitz: Hasidic tale as told by Chaim Stern in *Day by Day: Reflections on the Themes of the Torah from Literature, Philosophy and Religious Thought* (Boston: Beacon Press, 2001), pp. 328–29.

My dear Cristina, one must not be obsessed with the idea of security: Ignazio Silone, *Bread and Wine* (New York: Signet Classic, 1988).

Chapter 3 (pp. 50–69)

We spent the night recounting: From Primo Levi, "Pesa<u>h</u>," in *Collected Poems,* translated by Ruth Feldman and Brian Swan (London: Faber and Faber, 1988).

In Europe before World War II: See Yaffa Eliach, *There Once Was a World: A 900-Year Chronicle of the Shtetl of Eishyshok* (Boston: Little, Brown and Company, 1998), p. 431.

Judith Wallerstein wrote that the first task of any marriage: The Good Marriage, p. 55. (See Suggestions for Further Reading.)

Abraham … kept his tent: See *Bereshit Rabbah* 48:9. For many rabbinic teachings related to hospitality, see Hayim Nahman Bialik and Yehoshua Hana Ravnitsky, *The Book of Legends: Legends from the Talmud and Midrash* (New York: Schocken, 1992), pp. 679–82.

But it would not surprise Barry Schwartz: His most recent book on this topic is *The Paradox of Choice: Why More Is Less* (New York: Ecco, 2004).

Different explanations for the ingredients of <u>h</u>aroset: See Noam Zion and David Dishon, *Reader's Guide to the Family Participation Haggadah: A Different Night* (Jerusalem: Hartman Institute, 1997), pp. 12–13.

Hope is the thing that is left us in a bad time: Dorothy Lobrano, ed. *Letters of E. B. White* (New York: Harper and Row, 1976), p. 647.

A good relationship has a pattern: Anne Morrow Lindbergh, *Gift from the Sea* (New York: Pantheon, 1955), p. 104.

Chapter 4 (pp. 70–87)

I know how to dream: Elie Wiesel, *Gates of the Forest* (New York: Schocken, 1995), p. 211 (adapted).

Shavuot became linked with Sinai: Shabbat 86b.

Relationship between God and Israel as a marriage: Hosea, Jeremiah, Ezekiel, and Isaiah all used the imagery of God and Israel as husband and wife in their writings.

Wedding day of God and Israel: For further information about how this fits into the kabbalistic system, see Gershom Scholem, *Kabbalah and Its Symbolism* (New York: Schocken, 1969).

Preparing ethical wills: For a scholarly treatment of ethical wills among Jews, see Israel Abrahams, *Hebrew Ethical Wills* (Philadelphia: Jewish Publication Society, 1976). For a practical guide to the practice, see Jack Riemer and Nathaniel Stampfer, *So That Your Values Live On: Ethical Wills and How to Prepare Them* (Woodstock, VT: Jewish Lights Publishing, 2000).

Chapter 5 (pp. 88–105)

I have perceiv'd: Walt Whitman, "I Sing the Body Electric," *Leaves of Grass* (New York: Signet Classics, 2000).

Days are like scrolls: Baḥya Ibn Pekuda, *Duties of the Heart* (New York: Feldheim, 1978).

Join a community: Samson Raphael Hirsch, *The Nineteen Letters of Ben Uziel,* translated by B. Drachman (New York: Funk & Wagnalls, 1899).

Before creating the world: Midrash based on *Bereshit Rabbah* 3:7, as told by Chaim Stern, in *Day by Day: Reflections on the Themes of the Torah from Literature, Philosophy and Religious Thought* (Boston: Beacon Press, 2000), p. 1.

All changes, even the most longed for: A widely cited quote from Anatole France, "The Crime of Sylvestre Bonnard," *The Definitive Collection,* Part II (New York: Dodd-Mead, 1918), pp. 304–305.

Hineini: For more on this topic, see Norman J. Cohen, *Hineini in Our Lives: Learning How to Respond to Others through 14 Biblical Texts and Personal Stories* (Woodstock, VT: Jewish Lights Publishing, 2003).

Experience teaches us that love: From Antoine de Saint-Exupery, *Wind, Sand, and Stars* (London: Penguin Books, 1995), p. 110.

Human beings need but one book in their life: From Amir Gilboa, "Human Beings Need," as translated in *Kol HaNeshama: Prayerbook for the Days of Awe* (New York: The Reconstructionist Press, 1999), p. 26.

Chapter 6 (pp. 106–125)

Come back, come back: Shems Friedlander, *Rumi: The Hidden Treasure* (Louisville, KY: Fons Vitae, 2001).

Deborah Tannen: For a linguistic discussion of gender and conversation, see her book *You Just Don't Understand: Women and Men in Conversation* (New York: William Morrow, 1990).

There is a land of the living and a land of the dead: Thornton Wilder, *The Bridge of San Luis Rey* (New York: Albert and Charles Boni, 1927), p. 235.

The most unnoticed of all miracles: Moral Grandeur and Spiritual Audacity: Essays by Abraham Joshua Heschel, ed. Susannah Heschel (New York: Farrar, Straus and Giroux, 1997), p. 69.

Michael Ignatieff: Michael Ignatieff is a political philosopher and director of the Carr Center of Human Rights Policy.

Justice Ruth Bader Ginsburg: This story is found in Marlo Thomas, *The Right Words at the Right Time* (New York: Atria, 2002), p. 115.

Two rabbis once watched a colleague: Jewish stories are told and retold in a variety of versions. You can find one telling of this Hasidic tale in Shlomo Carlebach, *Shlomo's Stories* (Northvale, NJ: Jason Aronson, 1996), pp. 105–12. There are quite a few other great collections of Hasidic stories. We especially recommend Martin Buber, *Tales of the Hasidim* (two volumes) (New York: Schocken, 1991).

Rabbi Joseph Soloveitchik: For more reflections by Soloveitchik on repentance, see Pinchas H. Peli, *Soloveitchik on Repentance* (New York: Paulist Press, 1984).

Sefer Maalot HaMiddot: Eugene Borowitz used this classic list to organize a contemporary collection of practical ethical wisdom. See Eugene

B. Borowitz and Frances Weinman Schwartz, *The Jewish Moral Virtues* (Philadelphia: Jewish Publication Society, 1999).

Chapter 7 (pp. 126–139)

To live in this world: Mary Oliver, from "Blackwater Woods," in *New and Selected Poems* (Boston: Beacon, 2004).

Hallel: Traditionally, during Sukkot, Pesah, Shavuot, Hanukkah, and Rosh Hodesh (New Moon), the daily synagogue service includes the singing of Psalms 113–118, known as Psalms of Praise, or *Hallel.*

Living wills: For a wonderful resource go to the website of CLAL—The National Jewish Center for Learning and Leadership at www.simple-wisdom/secure/form/palcare.cfm, and order a copy of "Embracing Life & Facing Death: A Jewish Guide to Palliative Care."

O my love: From Marge Piercy, *The Art of Blessing the Day: Poems with a Jewish Theme* (New York: Random House USA, 2001).

Teach us how short: This is an adaptation of Psalm 90 written by Stephen Mitchell, found in his collection *A Book of Psalms: Selected and Adapted from the Hebrew* (San Francisco: HarperCollins, 1994).

People associate love with sentimental feeling alone: Herbert Weiner, "Rav Kuk's Path for Peace Within Israel," in *Commentary* 17, no. 3 (1954): 258.

Chapter 8 (pp. 140–159)

As the Torah scroll is read aloud: Yehudah Amichai, *Open, Closed, Open,* translated by Bloch and Kronfeld (New York: Harcourt, 2000).

We fight to keep warm: Barbara Myerhoff, *Number Our Days: A Triumph of Continuity and Culture among Jewish Old People in an Urban Ghetto* (New York: Simon & Schuster, 1978), p. 153.

Rabbi Dayle Friedman: From her book *Jewish Pastoral Care: A Practical Handbook from Traditional and Contemporary Sources* (Woodstock, VT: Jewish Lights Publishing, 2001).

The statement "If I can't dance, I don't want to be in your revolution": From *Women's Review of Books, 9,* no. 3 (December 1991).

Robert Coles recalls: From his book *The Call of Stories: Teaching and the Moral Imagination* (New York: Houghton Mifflin, 1989), p. xii.

Your life together is both circular and linear: For a book-length scholarly discussion of this issue, see Eliezer Schweid, *The Jewish Experience of Time* (Northvale, NJ: Jason Aronson, 2000).

Around the eleventh century: From the *Encyclopedia Judaica,* vol. 14 (Jerusalem: Keter Publishing, 1972), p. 1,571.

Mordecai Kaplan described: From Mordecai Kaplan, *Not So Random Thoughts* (New York: Jewish Reconstructionist Foundation, 1966), p. 282.

In my own worst seasons: Barbara Kingsolver, *High Tide in Tucson* (New York: HarperCollins, 1995), p. 15.

Just as the Torah is rolled: This prayer was written by Jill Hammer and can be found on the Web at www.ritualwell.org.

The way of Torah requires: From Rami Shapiro, *Wisdom of the Jewish Sages: A Modern Reading of Pirkei Avot* (New York: Harmony/Bell Tower, 1995).

The best thing for being sad: From T. H. White, *The Once and Future King* (New York: Berkeley Medallion Edition, 1966), p. 183.

Chapter 9 (pp. 160–177)

Three generations back: Marcia Lee Falk, "Will," in *The Book of Blessings: New Jewish Prayers for Daily Life, the Sabbath, and the New Moon Festival* (San Francisco: HarperSanFrancisco, 1996).

We have more timesaving devices: For a discussion of the acceleration of modern life, see James Gleick, *Faster: The Acceleration of Just About Everything* (New York: Pantheon, 1999).

Jenny and Sam always made sure not to use a knife: This custom is described for the first time in Richard Siegel, Michael Strassfeld, and Sharon Strassfeld, *The First Jewish Catalogue* (Philadelphia: Jewish Publication Society, 1973), p. 38.

In an eighteenth-century prayer book: Siddur Bet Yaakov, 158Aff. This prayer book is only available in Hebrew, but quotations from it can be found in Michael Kaufman, *Love, Marriage and Family in Jewish Law and Tradition* (Northvale, NJ: Jason Aronson, 1992), p. 222.

Maggie and Ed fought about money: Rabbi Marcia Prager tells a similar story in her book *The Path of Blessing* (Woodstock, VT: Jewish Lights Publishing, 2003). Rabbi Prager's teaching may well be the origin of the story we heard.

We drown the candle in the little lake of wine: Marge Piercy, "Havdalah," *The Art of Blessing the Day: Poems with a Jewish Theme* (New York: Knopf, 1999).

Afterword (pp. 179–180)

I can only answer the question: Alasdair MacIntyre, *After Virtue,* 2nd ed. (South Bend, IN: University of Notre Dame Press, 1984), p. 216.

Suggestions for Further Reading

Jewish Holidays & Ritual

Cardin, Nina Beth. *The Tapestry of Jewish Time: A Spiritual Guide to Holidays and Life-Cycle Events*. Springfield, NJ: Behrman House, 2000.

Greenberg, Blu. *How to Run a Traditional Jewish Household*. Northvale, NJ: Jason Aronson, 1989.

Greenberg, Irving. *The Jewish Way: Living the Jewish Holidays*. Northvale, NJ: Jason Aronson, 1998.

Heschel, Abraham Joshua. *The Sabbath*. Boston: Shambhala, 2003.

Kula, Irwin, and Vanessa Ochs. *The Book of Jewish Sacred Practices: KLAL's Guide to Everyday and Holiday Rituals and Blessings*. Woodstock, VT: Jewish Lights Publishing, 2001.

Milgram, Goldie. *Reclaiming Judaism as a Spiritual Practice: Holy Days and Shabbat*. Woodstock, VT: Jewish Lights Publishing, 2004.

Milgram, Goldie. *Meaning & Mitzvah: Daily Practices for Reclaiming Judaism through God, Torah, Mitzvot, Hebrew, Prayer, and Peoplehood*. Woodstock, VT: Jewish Lights Publishing, 2005.

Mykoff, Moshe. *7th Heaven: Celebrating Shabbat with Rebbe Nachman of Breslov*. Woodstock, VT: Jewish Lights Publishing, 2003.

Prager, Marcia. *The Path of Blessing: Experiencing the Energy and Abundance of the Divine*. Woodstock, VT: Jewish Lights Publishing, 2003.

Olitzky, Kerry M., and Daniel Judson. *The Rituals and Practices of a Jewish Life: A Handbook for Personal Spiritual Renewal*. Woodstock, VT: Jewish Lights Publishing, 2002.

Strassfeld, Michael. *The Jewish Holidays: A Guide and Commentary*. New York: HarperResource, 1993.

Waskow, Arthur. *Seasons of Our Joy: A Modern Guide to the Jewish Holidays*. Boston: Beacon Press, 1991.

Wolfson, Ron. _Hanukkah: The Family Guide to Spiritual Celebration_. Woodstock, VT: Jewish Lights Publishing, 2001.

———. _Passover: The Family Guide to Spiritual Celebration_. Woodstock, VT: Jewish Lights Publishing, 2002.

———. _Shabbat: The Family Guide to Preparing for and Celebrating the Sabbath_. Woodstock, VT: Jewish Lights Publishing, 2002.

Zion, Noam Sachs, and Shawn Fields-Mayer. _A Day Apart: Shabbat at Home_. Jerusalem: Shalom Hartman Institute, 2004.

Marriage and Relationships

Beck, Aaron T. _Love Is Never Enough: How Couples Can Overcome Misunderstandings, Resolve Conflicts, and Solve Relationship Problems through Cognitive Therapy_. New York: Harper & Row, 1989.

Cohen, Norman J. _Hineini in Our Lives: Learning How to Respond to Others through 14 Biblical Texts & Personal Stories_. Woodstock, VT: Jewish Lights Publishing, 2003.

———. _Self, Struggle & Change: Family Conflict Stories in Genesis and Their Healing Insights for Our Lives_. Woodstock, VT: Jewish Lights Publishing, 1995.

Crohn, Joel, Howard Markman, Janice R. Levine, and Susan L. Blumberg. _Fighting for Your Jewish Marriage: Preserving a Lasting Promise_. San Francisco: Jossey-Bass, 2001.

Friedland, Ronnie, and Edmund Case. _The Guide to Jewish Interfaith Family Life: An InterfaithFamily.com Handbook_. Woodstock, VT: Jewish Lights Publishing, 2001.

Gottman, John. _Why Marriages Succeed or Fail ... And How You Can Make Yours Last_. New York: Simon & Schuster, 1995.

Kellerman, Lois, and Nellie Bly. _Marriage from the Heart: Eight Commitments of a Spiritually Fulfilling Life Together_. New York: Penguin, 2003.

Lerner, Harriet. _The Dance of Anger: A Woman's Guide to Changing the Patterns of Intimate Relationships_. New York: Quill, 1997.

Olitzky, Kerry, M. _Introducing My Faith and My Community: The Jewish Outreach Institute Guide for the Christian in an Interfaith Relationship_. Woodstock, VT: Jewish Lights Publishing, 2004.

———. *Making a Successful Jewish Interfaith Marriage: The Jewish Outreach Institute Guide to Opportunities, Challenges, and Resources.* Woodstock, VT: Jewish Lights Publishing, 2000.

Orenstein, Debra. *Lifecycles, Vol. 1: Jewish Women on Life Passages and Personal Milestones.* Woodstock, VT: Jewish Lights Publishing, 1994.

Orenstein, Debra, and Jane Rachel Litman. *Lifecycles, Vol. 2: Jewish Women on Biblical Themes in Contemporary Life.* Woodstock, VT: Jewish Lights Publishing, 2000.

Page, Susan. *How One of You Can Bring the Two of You Together: Breakthrough Strategies to Resolve Your Conflicts and Reignite Your Love.* New York: Broadway Books, 1998.

Scarf, Maggie. *Intimate Partners: Patterns in Love and Marriage.* New York: Ballantine Books, 1996.

Tannen, Deborah. *"I Only Say This Because I Love You": How the Way We Talk Can Make or Break Family Relationships Throughout Our Lives.* New York: Ballantine, 2002.

Wallerstein, Judith, and Sandra Blakeslee. *The Good Marriage: How and Why Love Lasts.* New York: Warner Books, 1996.

Credits

"The Layers," from *The Collected Poems of Stanley Kunitz,* © 2000 by Stanley Kunitz (New York: W. W. Norton & Company, 2002). Used by permission of W. W. Norton & Company, Inc.

"My Mother's Body," from *My Mother's Body* by Marge Piercy, © 1985 by Marge Piercy. Used by permission of Alfred A. Knopf, a division of Random House, Inc.

"The Art of Blessing the Day," from *The Art of Blessing the Day* by Marge Piercy, © 1999 by Middlemarsh, Inc. Used by permission of Alfred A. Knopf, a division of Random House, Inc.

"Human Beings in Need," by Amir Gilboa, translated in *Kol Haneshamah: Mahzor Leyamim Nora'im* (Elkins Park, PA: The Reconstructionist Press, 1999). Used by permission.

"Come back, come back," from *Rumi: The Hidden Treasure,* translated by Shems Friedlander (Louisville, KY: Fons Vitae, 2001). Used by permission.

"Will," © 1996 by Marcia Lee Falk. From *The Book of Blessings: New Jewish Prayers for Daily Life, the Sabbath, and the New Moon Festival* by Marcia Lee Falk (San Francisco: HarperSanFrancisco, 1996; paperback edition, Boston: Beacon Press, 1999). Used by permission of the author.

From "Blackwater Woods," from *New and Selected Poems* by Mary Oliver (Boston: Beacon Press, 2004). Used by permission.

Every effort has been made to trace and acknowledge copyright holders of all excerpts. The authors apologize for any errors or omissions that may remain, and ask that any omissions be brought to their attention so that they may be corrected in future editions.

Bar/Bat Mitzvah

The JGirl's Guide: The Young Jewish Woman's Handbook for Coming of Age
By Penina Adelman, Ali Feldman, and Shulamit Reinharz
An inspirational, interactive guidebook designed to help pre-teen Jewish girls address the spiritual, educational, and psychological issues surrounding coming of age in today's society. 6 x 9, 240 pp, Quality PB, ISBN 1-58023-215-9 **$14.99**

Bar/Bat Mitzvah Basics: A Practical Family Guide to Coming of Age Together
By Helen Leneman 6 x 9, 240 pp, Quality PB, ISBN 1-58023-151-9 **$18.95**

The Bar/Bat Mitzvah Memory Book: An Album for Treasuring the Spiritual Celebration
By Rabbi Jeffrey K. Salkin and Nina Salkin
8 x 10, 48 pp, Deluxe Hardcover, 2-color text, ribbon marker, ISBN 1-58023-111-X **$19.95**

For Kids—Putting God on Your Guest List: How to Claim the Spiritual Meaning of Your Bar or Bat Mitzvah *By Rabbi Jeffrey K. Salkin*
6 x 9, 144 pp, Quality PB, ISBN 1-58023-015-6 **$14.99** *For ages 11–12*

Putting God on the Guest List, 3rd Edition: How to Reclaim the Spiritual Meaning of Your Child's Bar or Bat Mitzvah *By Rabbi Jeffrey K. Salkin*
6 x 9, 224 pp, Quality PB, ISBN 1-58023-222-1 **$16.99**; Hardcover, ISBN 1-58023-260-4 **$24.99**

Tough Questions Jews Ask: A Young Adult's Guide to Building a Jewish Life
By Rabbi Edward Feinstein 6 x 9, 160 pp, Quality PB, ISBN 1-58023-139-X **$14.99** *For ages 13 & up*
Also Available: **Tough Questions Jews Ask Teacher's Guide**
8½ x 11, 72 pp, PB, ISBN 1-58023-187-X **$8.95**

Bible Study/Midrash

Hineini in Our Lives: Learning How to Respond to Others through 14 Biblical Texts, and Personal Stories *By Norman J. Cohen* 6 x 9, 240 pp, Hardcover, ISBN 1-58023-131-4 **$23.95**

Ancient Secrets: Using the Stories of the Bible to Improve Our Everyday Lives
By Rabbi Levi Meier, Ph.D. 5½ x 8½, 288 pp, Quality PB, ISBN 1-58023-064-4 **$16.95**

Moses—The Prince, the Prophet: His Life, Legend & Message for Our Lives
By Rabbi Levi Meier, Ph.D. 6 x 9, 224 pp, Quality PB, ISBN 1-58023-069-5 **$16.95**

Self, Struggle & Change: Family Conflict Stories in Genesis and Their Healing Insights for Our Lives *By Norman J. Cohen* 6 x 9, 224 pp, Quality PB, ISBN 1-879045-66-4 **$18.99**

Voices from Genesis: Guiding Us through the Stages of Life *By Norman J. Cohen*
6 x 9, 192 pp, Quality PB, ISBN 1-58023-118-7 **$16.95**

Congregation Resources

Becoming a Congregation of Learners: Learning as a Key to Revitalizing Congregational Life *By Isa Aron, Ph.D. Foreword by Rabbi Lawrence A. Hoffman.*
6 x 9, 304 pp, Quality PB, ISBN 1-58023-089-X **$19.95**

Finding a Spiritual Home: How a New Generation of Jews Can Transform the American Synagogue *By Rabbi Sidney Schwarz*
6 x 9, 352 pp, Quality PB, ISBN 1-58023-185-3 **$19.95**

Jewish Pastoral Care, 2nd Edition: A Practical Handbook from Traditional & Contemporary Sources *Edited by Rabbi Dayle A. Friedman*
6 x 9, 464 pp, Hardcover, ISBN 1-58023-221-3 **$40.00**

The Self-Renewing Congregation: Organizational Strategies for Revitalizing Congregational Life *By Isa Aron, Ph.D. Foreword by Dr. Ron Wolfson.*
6 x 9, 304 pp, Quality PB, ISBN 1-58023-166-7 **$19.95**

Or phone, fax, mail or e-mail to: **JEWISH LIGHTS Publishing**
Sunset Farm Offices, Route 4 • P.O. Box 237 • Woodstock, Vermont 05091
Tel: (802) 457-4000 • Fax: (802) 457-4004 • www.jewishlights.com
Credit card orders: (800) 962-4544 (8:30AM–5:30PM ET Monday–Friday)
Generous discounts on quantity orders. SATISFACTION GUARANTEED. Prices subject to change.

Children's Books

What You Will See Inside a Synagogue
By Rabbi Lawrence A. Hoffman and Dr. Ron Wolfson; Full-color photos by Bill Aron
A colorful, fun-to-read introduction that explains the ways and whys of Jewish worship and religious life. Full-page photos; concise but informative descriptions of the objects used, the clergy and laypeople who have specific roles, and much more. For ages 6 & up.
8½ x 10½, 32 pp, Full-color photos, Hardcover, ISBN 1-59473-012-1 **$17.99** *(A SkyLight Paths book)*

Because Nothing Looks Like God
By Lawrence and Karen Kushner
What is God like? Introduces children to the possibilities of spiritual life. Real-life examples of happiness and sadness invite us to explore, together with our children, the questions we all have about God.
11 x 8½, 32 pp, Full-color illus., Hardcover, ISBN 1-58023-092-X **$16.95** *For ages 4 & up*

Also Available: **Because Nothing Looks Like God Teacher's Guide**
8½ x 11, 22 pp, PB, ISBN 1-58023-140-3 **$6.95** *For ages 5–8*

Board Book Companions to *Because Nothing Looks Like God*
5 x 5, 24 pp, Full-color illus., SkyLight Paths Board Books, **$7.95** each *For ages 0–4*

What Does God Look Like? ISBN 1-893361-23-3

How Does God Make Things Happen? ISBN 1-893361-24-1

Where Is God? ISBN 1-893361-17-9

The 11th Commandment: Wisdom from Our Children
by The Children of America
"If there were an Eleventh Commandment, what would it be?" Children of many religious denominations across America answer in their own drawings and words.
8 x 10, 48 pp, Full-color illus., Hardcover, ISBN 1-879045-46-X **$16.95** *For all ages*

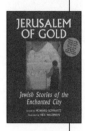

Jerusalem of Gold: Jewish Stories of the Enchanted City
Retold by Howard Schwartz. Full-color illus. by Neil Waldman.
A beautiful and engaging collection of historical and legendary stories for children. Based on Talmud, midrash, Jewish folklore, and mystical and Hasidic sources.
8 x 10, 64 pp, Full-color illus., Hardcover, ISBN 1-58023-149-7 **$18.95** *For ages 7 & up*

The Book of Miracles: A Young Person's Guide to Jewish Spiritual Awareness
By Lawrence Kushner. All-new illustrations by the author.
6 x 9, 96 pp, 2-color illus., Hardcover, ISBN 1-879045-78-8 **$16.95** *For ages 9–13*

In Our Image: God's First Creatures
By Nancy Sohn Swartz
9 x 12, 32 pp, Full-color illus., Hardcover, ISBN 1-879045-99-0 **$16.95** *For ages 4 & up*

Also Available as a Board Book: **How Did the Animals Help God?**
5 x 5, 24 pp, Board, Full-color illus., ISBN 1-59473-044-X **$7.99** *For ages 0–4 (A SkyLight Paths book)*

From SKYLIGHT PATHS PUBLISHING

Becoming Me: A Story of Creation
By Martin Boroson. Full-color illus. by Christopher Gilvan-Cartwright.
Told in the personal "voice" of the Creator, a story about creation and relationship that is about each one of us.
8 x 10, 32 pp, Full-color illus., Hardcover, ISBN 1-893361-11-X **$16.95** *For ages 4 & up*

Ten Amazing People: And How They Changed the World
By Maura D. Shaw. Foreword by Dr. Robert Coles. Full-color illus. by Stephen Marchesi.
Black Elk • Dorothy Day • Malcolm X • Mahatma Gandhi • Martin Luther King, Jr. • Mother Teresa • Janusz Korczak • Desmond Tutu • Thich Nhat Hanh • Albert Schweitzer.
8½ x 11, 48 pp, Full-color illus., Hardcover, ISBN 1-893361-47-0 **$17.95** *For ages 7 & up*

Where Does God Live? *By August Gold and Matthew J. Perlman*
Helps young readers develop a personal understanding of God.
10 x 8½ , 32 pp, Full-color photo illus., Quality PB, ISBN 1-893361-39-X **$8.99** *For ages 3–6*

Abraham Joshua Heschel

The Earth Is the Lord's: The Inner World of the Jew in Eastern Europe
5½ x 8, 128 pp, Quality PB, ISBN 1-879045-42-7 **$14.95**

Israel: An Echo of Eternity *New Introduction by Susannah Heschel*
5½ x 8, 272 pp, Quality PB, ISBN 1-879045-70-2 **$19.95**

A Passion for Truth: Despair and Hope in Hasidism
5½ x 8, 352 pp, Quality PB, ISBN 1-879045-41-9 **$18.99**

Holidays/Holy Days

Leading the Passover Journey
The Seder's Meaning Revealed, the Haggadah's Story Retold
By Rabbi Nathan Laufer
Uncovers the hidden meaning of the Seder's rituals and customs
6 x 9, 208 pp, Hardcover, ISBN 1-58023-211-6 **$24.99**

Reclaiming Judaism as a Spiritual Practice: Holy Days and Shabbat
By Rabbi Goldie Milgram
Provides a framework for understanding the powerful and often unexplained intellectual, emotional, and spiritual tools that are essential for a lively, relevant, and fulfilling Jewish spiritual practice. 7 x 9, 272 pp, Quality PB, ISBN 1-58023-205-1 **$19.99**

7th Heaven: Celebrating Shabbat with Rebbe Nachman of Breslov
By Moshe Mykoff with the Breslov Research Institute
Explores the art of consciously observing Shabbat and understanding in-depth many of the day's spiritual practices. 5⅛ x 8¼, 224 pp, Deluxe PB w/flaps, ISBN 1-58023-175-6 **$18.95**

The Women's Passover Companion
Women's Reflections on the Festival of Freedom
Edited by Rabbi Sharon Cohen Anisfeld, Tara Mohr, and Catherine Spector
Groundbreaking. A provocative conversation about women's relationships to Passover as well as the roots and meanings of women's seders.
6 x 9, 352 pp, Hardcover, ISBN 1-58023-128-4 **$24.95**

The Women's Seder Sourcebook
Rituals & Readings for Use at the Passover Seder
Edited by Rabbi Sharon Cohen Anisfeld, Tara Mohr, and Catherine Spector
Gathers the voices of more than one hundred women in readings, personal and creative reflections, commentaries, blessings, and ritual suggestions that can be incorporated into your Passover celebration.
6 x 9, 384 pp, Hardcover, ISBN 1-58023-136-5 **$24.95**

Creating Lively Passover Seders: A Sourcebook of Engaging Tales, Texts & Activities
By David Arnow, Ph.D. 7 x 9, 416 pp, Quality PB, ISBN 1-58023-184-5 **$24.99**

Hanukkah, 2nd Edition: The Family Guide to Spiritual Celebration
By Dr. Ron Wolfson. Edited by Joel Lurie Grishaver.
7 x 9, 240 pp, illus., Quality PB, ISBN 1-58023-122-5 **$18.95**

The Jewish Family Fun Book: Holiday Projects, Everyday Activities, and Travel Ideas
with Jewish Themes *By Danielle Dardashti and Roni Sarig. Illus. by Avi Katz.*
6 x 9, 288 pp, 70+ b/w illus. & diagrams, Quality PB, ISBN 1-58023-171-3 **$18.95**

The Jewish Gardening Cookbook: Growing Plants & Cooking for
Holidays & Festivals *By Michael Brown* 6 x 9, 224 pp, 30+ illus., Quality PB, ISBN 1-58023-116-0 **$16.95**

The Jewish Lights Book of Fun Classroom Activities: Simple and Seasonal
Projects for Teachers and Students *By Danielle Dardashti and Roni Sarig*
6 x 9, 240 pp, Quality PB, ISBN 1–58023–206–X **$19.99**

Passover, 2nd Edition: The Family Guide to Spiritual Celebration
By Dr. Ron Wolfson with Joel Lurie Grishaver 7 x 9, 352 pp, Quality PB, ISBN 1-58023-174-8 **$19.95**

Shabbat, 2nd Edition: The Family Guide to Preparing for and Celebrating the Sabbath
By Dr. Ron Wolfson 7 x 9, 320 pp, illus., Quality PB, ISBN 1-58023-164-0 **$19.95**

Sharing Blessings: Children's Stories for Exploring the Spirit of the Jewish Holidays
By Rahel Musleah and Michael Klayman
8½ x 11, 64 pp, Full-color illus., Hardcover, ISBN 1-879045-71-0 **$18.95** *For ages 6 & up*

Inspiration

God in All Moments
Mystical & Practical Spiritual Wisdom from Hasidic Masters
Edited and translated by Or N. Rose with Ebn D. Leader
Hasidic teachings on how to be mindful in religious practice and cultivating every-day ethical behavior—*hanhagot*. 5½ x 8¼, 192 pp, Quality PB, ISBN 1-58023-186-1 **$16.95**

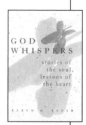

Our Dance with God: Finding Prayer, Perspective and Meaning in the
Stories of Our Lives *By Karyn D. Kedar*
Inspiring spiritual insight to guide you on your life journeys and teach you to live and thrive in two conflicting worlds: the rational/material and the spiritual.
6 x 9, 176 pp, Quality PB, ISBN 1-58023-202-7 **$16.99**

Also Available: **The Dance of the Dolphin** (Hardcover edition of *Our Dance with God*)
6 x 9, 176 pp, Hardcover, ISBN 1-58023-154-3 **$19.95**

The Empty Chair: Finding Hope and Joy—Timeless Wisdom from a Hasidic Master,
Rebbe Nachman of Breslov *Adapted by Moshe Mykoff and the Breslov Research Institute*
4 x 6, 128 pp, 2-color text, Deluxe PB w/flaps, ISBN 1-879045-67-2 **$9.95**

The Gentle Weapon: Prayers for Everyday and Not-So-Everyday Moments—
Timeless Wisdom from the Teachings of the Hasidic Master, Rebbe Nachman of Breslov
Adapted by Moshe Mykoff and S. C. Mizrahi, together with the Breslov Research Institute
4 x 6, 144 pp, 2-color text, Deluxe PB w/flaps, ISBN 1-58023-022-9 **$9.95**

God Whispers: Stories of the Soul, Lessons of the Heart *By Karyn D. Kedar*
6 x 9, 176 pp, Quality PB, ISBN 1-58023-088-1 **$15.95**

An Orphan in History: One Man's Triumphant Search for His Jewish Roots
By Paul Cowan. Afterword by Rachel Cowan. 6 x 9, 288 pp, Quality PB, ISBN 1-58023-135-7 **$16.95**

Restful Reflections: Nighttime Inspiration to Calm the Soul, Based on Jewish Wisdom
By Rabbi Kerry M. Olitzky & Rabbi Lori Forman 4½ x 6¼, 448 pp, Quality PB, ISBN 1-58023-091-1 **$15.95**

Sacred Intentions: Daily Inspiration to Strengthen the Spirit, Based on Jewish Wisdom
By Rabbi Kerry M. Olitzky and Rabbi Lori Forman 4½ x 6¼, 448 pp, Quality PB, ISBN 1-58023-061-X **$15.95**

Kabbalah/Mysticism/Enneagram

Seek My Face: A Jewish Mystical Theology
By Dr. Arthur Green
This classic work of contemporary Jewish theology, revised and updated, is a pro-found, deeply personal statement of the lasting truths of Jewish mysticism and the basic faith claims of Judaism. A tool for anyone seeking the elusive presence of God in the world. 6 x 9, 304 pp, Quality PB, ISBN 1-58023-130-6 **$19.95**

Zohar: Annotated & Explained
Translation and annotation by Dr. Daniel C. Matt. Foreword by Andrew Harvey
Offers insightful yet unobtrusive commentary to the masterpiece of Jewish mys-ticism. Explains references and mystical symbols, shares wisdom of spiritual mas-ters, and clarifies the *Zohar*'s bold claim: We have always been taught that we need God, but in order to manifest in the world, God needs us.
5½ x 8¼, 160 pp, Quality PB, ISBN 1-893361-51-9 **$15.99** *(A SkyLight Paths book)*

Cast in God's Image: Discover Your Personality Type Using the Enneagram and Kabbalah
By Rabbi Howard A. Addison
7 x 9, 176 pp, Quality PB, Layflat binding, 20+ journaling exercises, ISBN 1-58023-124-1 **$16.95**

Ehyeh: A Kabbalah for Tomorrow *By Dr. Arthur Green*
6 x 9, 224 pp, Quality PB, ISBN 1-58023-213-2 **$16.99;** Hardcover, ISBN 1-58023-125-X **$21.95**

The Enneagram and Kabbalah: Reading Your Soul *By Rabbi Howard A. Addison*
6 x 9, 176 pp, Quality PB, ISBN 1-58023-001-6 **$15.95**

Finding Joy: A Practical Spiritual Guide to Happiness *By Dannel I. Schwartz with Mark Hass*
6 x 9, 192 pp, Quality PB, ISBN 1-58023-009-1 **$14.95**

The Gift of Kabbalah: Discovering the Secrets of Heaven, Renewing Your Life on Earth
By Tamar Frankiel, Ph.D.
6 x 9, 256 pp, Quality PB, ISBN 1-58023-141-1 **$16.95;** Hardcover, ISBN 1-58023-108-X **$21.95**

The Way Into Jewish Mystical Tradition *By Lawrence Kushner*
6 x 9, 224 pp, Quality PB, ISBN 1-58023-200-0 **$18.99;** Hardcover, ISBN 1-58023-029-6 **$21.95**

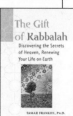

Life Cycle

Marriage / Parenting / Family / Aging

Jewish Fathers: A Legacy of Love
Photographs by Lloyd Wolf. Essays by Paula Wolfson. Foreword by Harold S. Kushner.
Honors the role of contemporary Jewish fathers in America. Each father tells in his own words what it means to be a parent and Jewish, and what he learned from his own father. Insightful photos. 9½ x 9⅞, 144 pp with 100+ duotone photos, Hardcover, ISBN 1-58023-204-3 **$30.00**

The New Jewish Baby Album: Creating and Celebrating the Beginning of a Spiritual Life—A Jewish Lights Companion
By the Editors at Jewish Lights. Foreword by Anita Diamant. Preface by Sandy Eisenberg Sasso.
A spiritual keepsake that will be treasured for generations. More than just a memory book, *shows you how—and why it's important*—to create a Jewish home and a Jewish life. 8 x 10, 64 pp, Deluxe Padded Hardcover, Full-color illus., ISBN 1-58023-138-1 **$19.95**

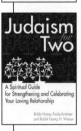

The Jewish Pregnancy Book: A Resource for the Soul, Body & Mind during Pregnancy, Birth & the First Three Months
By Sandy Falk, M.D., and Rabbi Daniel Judson, with Steven A. Rapp
Includes medical information, prayers and rituals for each stage of pregnancy, from a liberal Jewish perspective. 7 x 10, 208 pp, Quality PB, b/w illus., ISBN 1-58023-178-0 **$16.95**

Celebrating Your New Jewish Daughter: Creating Jewish Ways to Welcome Baby Girls into the Covenant—New and Traditional Ceremonies
By Debra Nussbaum Cohen 6 x 9, 272 pp, Quality PB, ISBN 1-58023-090-3 **$18.95**

The New Jewish Baby Book, 2nd Edition: Names, Ceremonies & Customs—A Guide for Today's Families *By Anita Diamant* 6 x 9, 336 pp, Quality PB, ISBN 1-58023-251-5 **$19.99**

Parenting As a Spiritual Journey: Deepening Ordinary and Extraordinary Events into Sacred Occasions *By Rabbi Nancy Fuchs-Kreimer* 6 x 9, 224 pp, Quality PB, ISBN 1-58023-016-4 **$16.95**

Judaism for Two: A Spiritual Guide for Strengthening and Celebrating Your Loving Relationship *By Rabbi Nancy Fuchs-Kreimer and Rabbi Nancy H. Wiener*
Addresses the ways Jewish teachings can enhance and strengthen committed relationships. 6 x 9, 208 pp, Quality PB, ISBN 1-58023-254-X **$16.99**

Embracing the Covenant: Converts to Judaism Talk About Why & How
By Rabbi Allan Berkowitz and Patti Moskovitz 6 x 9, 192 pp, Quality PB, ISBN 1-879045-50-8 **$16.95**

The Guide to Jewish Interfaith Family Life: An InterfaithFamily.com Handbook
Edited by Ronnie Friedland and Edmund Case 6 x 9, 384 pp, Quality PB, ISBN 1-58023-153-5 **$18.95**

Introducing My Faith and My Community
The Jewish Outreach Institute Guide for the Christian in a Jewish Interfaith Relationship
By Rabbi Kerry M. Olitzky 6 x 9, 176 pp, Quality PB, ISBN 1-58023-192-6 **$16.99**

Making a Successful Jewish Interfaith Marriage: The Jewish Outreach Institute Guide to Opportunities, Challenges and Resources
By Rabbi Kerry M. Olitzky with Joan Peterson Littman 6 x 9, 176 pp, Quality PB, ISBN 1-58023-170-5 **$16.95**

The Creative Jewish Wedding Book: A Hands-On Guide to New & Old Traditions, Ceremonies & Celebrations *By Gabrielle Kaplan-Mayer*
Provides the tools to create the most meaningful Jewish traditional or alternative wedding by using ritual elements to express your unique style and spirituality. 9 x 9, 288 pp, b/w photos, Quality PB, ISBN 1-58023-194-2 **$19.99**

Divorce Is a Mitzvah: A Practical Guide to Finding Wholeness and Holiness When Your Marriage Dies *By Rabbi Perry Netter. Afterword by Rabbi Laura Geller.*
6 x 9, 224 pp, Quality PB, ISBN 1-58023-172-1 **$16.95**

A Heart of Wisdom: Making the Jewish Journey from Midlife through the Elder Years
Edited by Susan Berrin. Foreword by Harold Kushner. 6 x 9, 384 pp, Quality PB, ISBN 1-58023-051-2 **$18.95**

So That Your Values Live On: Ethical Wills and How to Prepare Them
Edited by Jack Riemer and Nathaniel Stampfer 6 x 9, 272 pp, Quality PB, ISBN 1-879045-34-6 **$18.95**

Meditation

The Handbook of Jewish Meditation Practices
A Guide for Enriching the Sabbath and Other Days of Your Life
By Rabbi David A. Cooper
Easy-to-learn meditation techniques. 6 x 9, 208 pp, Quality PB, ISBN 1-58023-102-0 **$16.95**

Discovering Jewish Meditation: Instruction & Guidance for Learning an Ancient
Spiritual Practice *By Nan Fink Gefen, Ph.D.* 6 x 9, 208 pp, Quality PB, ISBN 1-58023-067-9 **$16.95**

A Heart of Stillness: A Complete Guide to Learning the Art of Meditation
By Rabbi David A. Cooper 5½ x 8½, 272 pp, Quality PB, ISBN 1-893361-03-9 **$16.95**
(A SkyLight Paths book)

Meditation from the Heart of Judaism: Today's Teachers Share Their
Practices, Techniques, and Faith *Edited by Avram Davis*
6 x 9, 256 pp, Quality PB, ISBN 1-58023-049-0 **$16.95**

Silence, Simplicity & Solitude: A Complete Guide to Spiritual Retreat at Home
By Rabbi David A. Cooper 5½ x 8½, 336 pp, Quality PB, ISBN 1-893361-04-7 **$16.95**
(A SkyLight Paths book)

The Way of Flame: A Guide to the Forgotten Mystical Tradition of Jewish
Meditation *By Avram Davis* 4½ x 8, 176 pp, Quality PB, ISBN 1-58023-060-1 **$15.95**

Ritual/Sacred Practice/Journaling

The Jewish Dream Book: The Key to Opening the Inner Meaning of
Your Dreams *By Vanessa L. Ochs with Elizabeth Ochs; Full-color illus. by Kristina Swarner*
Instructions for how modern people can perform ancient Jewish dream practices
and dream interpretations drawn from the Jewish wisdom tradition. For anyone
who wants to understand their dreams—and themselves.
8 x 8, 120 pp, Full-color illus., Deluxe PB w/flaps, ISBN 1-58023-132-2 **$16.95**

The Jewish Journaling Book: How to Use Jewish Tradition to Write
Your Life & Explore Your Soul *By Janet Ruth Falon*
Details the history of Jewish journaling throughout biblical and modern times,
and teaches specific journaling techniques to help you create and maintain a vital
journal, from a Jewish perspective. 8 x 8, 304 pp, Deluxe PB w/flaps, ISBN 1-58023-203-5 **$18.99**

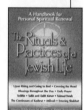

The Book of Jewish Sacred Practices: CLAL's Guide to Everyday & Holiday
Rituals & Blessings *Edited by Rabbi Irwin Kula and Vanessa L. Ochs, Ph.D.*
6 x 9, 368 pp, Quality PB, ISBN 1-58023-152-7 **$18.95**

Jewish Ritual: A Brief Introduction for Christians
By Rabbi Kerry M. Olitzky and Rabbi Daniel Judson
5½ x 8½, 144 pp, Quality PB, ISBN 1-58023-210-8 **$14.99**

The Rituals & Practices of a Jewish Life: A Handbook for Personal Spiritual
Renewal *Edited by Rabbi Kerry M. Olitzky and Rabbi Daniel Judson*
6 x 9, 272 pp, illus., Quality PB, ISBN 1-58023-169-1 **$18.95**

Science Fiction/ Mystery & Detective Fiction

Mystery Midrash: An Anthology of Jewish Mystery & Detective Fiction
Edited by Lawrence W. Raphael. Preface by Joel Siegel.
6 x 9, 304 pp, Quality PB, ISBN 1-58023-055-5 **$16.95**

Criminal Kabbalah: An Intriguing Anthology of Jewish Mystery & Detective Fiction
Edited by Lawrence W. Raphael. Foreword by Laurie R. King.
6 x 9, 256 pp, Quality PB, ISBN 1-58023-109-8 **$16.95**

More Wandering Stars: An Anthology of Outstanding Stories of Jewish Fantasy and
Science Fiction *Edited by Jack Dann. Introduction by Isaac Asimov.*
6 x 9, 192 pp, Quality PB, ISBN 1-58023-063-6 **$16.95**

Wandering Stars: An Anthology of Jewish Fantasy & Science Fiction
Edited by Jack Dann. Introduction by Isaac Asimov.
6 x 9, 272 pp, Quality PB, ISBN 1-58023-005-9 **$16.95**

Spirituality

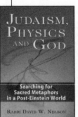

Does the Soul Survive?: A Jewish Journey to Belief in Afterlife, Past Lives & Living with Purpose *By Rabbi Elie Kaplan Spitz. Foreword by Brian L. Weiss, M.D.*
Spitz relates his own experiences and those shared with him by people he has worked with as a rabbi, and shows us that belief in afterlife and past lives, so often approached with reluctance, is in fact true to Jewish tradition.
6 x 9, 288 pp, Quality PB, ISBN 1-58023-165-9 **$16.95**; Hardcover, ISBN 1-58023-094-6 **$21.95**

First Steps to a New Jewish Spirit: Reb Zalman's Guide to Recapturing the Intimacy & Ecstasy in Your Relationship with God
By Rabbi Zalman M. Schachter-Shalomi with Donald Gropman
An extraordinary spiritual handbook that restores psychic and physical vigor by introducing us to new models and alternative ways of practicing Judaism. Offers meditation and contemplation exercises for enriching the most important aspects of everyday life.   6 x 9, 144 pp, Quality PB, ISBN 1-58023-182-9 **$16.95**

God in Our Relationships: Spirituality between People from the Teachings of Martin Buber   *By Rabbi Dennis S. Ross*
On the eightieth anniversary of Buber's classic work, we can discover new answers to critical issues in our lives. Inspiring examples from Ross's own life—as congregational rabbi, father, hospital chaplain, social worker, and husband—illustrate Buber's difficult-to-understand ideas about how we encounter God and each other. 5½ x 8½, 160 pp, Quality PB, ISBN 1-58023-147-0 **$16.95**

Judaism, Physics and God: Searching for Sacred Metaphors in a Post-Einstein World   *By Rabbi David W. Nelson*
In clear, non-technical terms, this provocative fusion of religion and science examines the great theories of modern physics to find new ways for contemporary people to express their spiritual beliefs and thoughts.
6 x 9, 352 pp, Hardcover, ISBN 1-58023-252-3 **$24.99**

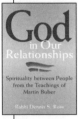

The Jewish Lights Spirituality Handbook: A Guide to Understanding, Exploring & Living a Spiritual Life   *Edited by Stuart M. Matlins*
What exactly is "Jewish" about spirituality? How do I make it a part of my life? Fifty of today's foremost spiritual leaders share their ideas and experience with us.
6 x 9, 456 pp, Quality PB, ISBN 1-58023-093-8 **$19.95**; Hardcover, ISBN 1-58023-100-4 **$24.95**

Bringing the Psalms to Life: How to Understand and Use the Book of Psalms
By Dr. Daniel F. Polish
6 x 9, 208 pp, Quality PB, ISBN 1-58023-157-8 **$16.95**; Hardcover, ISBN 1-58023-077-6 **$21.95**

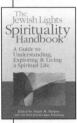

God & the Big Bang: Discovering Harmony between Science & Spirituality
By Dr. Daniel C. Matt 6 x 9, 216 pp, Quality PB, ISBN 1-879045-89-3 **$16.95**

Godwrestling—Round 2: Ancient Wisdom, Future Paths
By Rabbi Arthur Waskow 6 x 9, 352 pp, Quality PB, ISBN 1-879045-72-9 **$18.95**

One God Clapping: The Spiritual Path of a Zen Rabbi   *By Rabbi Alan Lew with Sherril Jaffe*
5½ x 8½, 336 pp, Quality PB, ISBN 1-58023-115-2 **$16.95**

The Path of Blessing: Experiencing the Energy and Abundance of the Divine
By Rabbi Marcia Prager 5½ x 8½, 240 pp., Quality PB, ISBN 1-58023-148-9 **$16.95**

Six Jewish Spiritual Paths: A Rationalist Looks at Spirituality   *By Rabbi Rifat Sonsino*
6 x 9, 208 pp, Quality PB, ISBN 1-58023-167-5 **$16.95**; Hardcover, ISBN 1-58023-095-4 **$21.95**

Soul Judaism: Dancing with God into a New Era
By Rabbi Wayne Dosick 5½ x 8½, 304 pp, Quality PB, ISBN 1-58023-053-9 **$16.95**

Stepping Stones to Jewish Spiritual Living: Walking the Path Morning, Noon, and Night *By Rabbi James L. Mirel and Karen Bonnell Werth*
6 x 9, 240 pp, Quality PB, ISBN 1-58023-074-1 **$16.95**; Hardcover, ISBN 1-58023-003-2 **$21.95**

There Is No Messiah... and You're It: The Stunning Transformation of Judaism's Most Provocative Idea *By Rabbi Robert N. Levine, D.D.*
6 x 9, 192 pp, Quality PB, ISBN 1-58023-255-8 **$16.99**; Hardcover, ISBN 1-58023-173-X **$21.95**

These Are the Words: A Vocabulary of Jewish Spiritual Life   *By Dr. Arthur Green*
6 x 9, 304 pp, Quality PB, ISBN 1-58023-107-1 **$18.95**

Spirituality/Lawrence Kushner

Filling Words with Light: Hasidic and Mystical Reflections on Jewish Prayer
By Lawrence Kushner and Nehemia Polen
Reflects on the joy, gratitude, mystery, and awe embedded in traditional prayers and blessings, and shows how you can imbue these familiar sacred words with your own sense of holiness. 5½ x 8½, 176 pp, Hardcover, ISBN 1-58023-216-7 **$21.99**

The Book of Letters: A Mystical Hebrew Alphabet
Popular Hardcover Edition, 6 x 9, 80 pp, 2-color text, ISBN 1-879045-00-1 **$24.95**
Collector's Limited Edition, 9 x 12, 80 pp, gold foil embossed pages, w/limited edition silkscreened print, ISBN 1-879045-04-4 **$349.00**

The Book of Miracles: A Young Person's Guide to Jewish Spiritual Awareness
6 x 9, 96 pp, 2-color illus., Hardcover, ISBN 1-879045-78-8 **$16.95** *For ages 9–13*

The Book of Words: Talking Spiritual Life, Living Spiritual Talk
6 x 9, 160 pp, Quality PB, ISBN 1-58023-020-2 **$16.95**

Eyes Remade for Wonder: A Lawrence Kushner Reader *Introduction by Thomas Moore*
6 x 9, 240 pp, Quality PB, ISBN 1-58023-042-3 **$18.95;** Hardcover, ISBN 1-58023-014-8 **$23.95**

God Was in This Place & I, i Did Not Know
Finding Self, Spirituality and Ultimate Meaning 6 x 9, 192 pp, Quality PB, ISBN 1-879045-33-8 **$16.95**

Honey from the Rock: An Introduction to Jewish Mysticism
6 x 9, 176 pp, Quality PB, ISBN 1-58023-073-3 **$16.95**

Invisible Lines of Connection: Sacred Stories of the Ordinary
5½ x 8½, 160 pp, Quality PB, ISBN 1-879045-98-2 **$15.95**

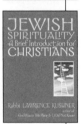

Jewish Spirituality—A Brief Introduction for Christians
5½ x 8½, 112 pp, Quality PB Original, ISBN 1-58023-150-0 **$12.95**

The River of Light: Jewish Mystical Awareness 6 x 9, 192 pp, Quality PB, ISBN 1-58023-096-2 **$16.95**

The Way Into Jewish Mystical Tradition
6 x 9, 224 pp, Quality PB, ISBN 1-58023-200-0 **$18.99;** Hardcover, ISBN 1-58023-029-6 **$21.95**

Spirituality/Prayer

Pray Tell: A Hadassah Guide to Jewish Prayer
By Rabbi Jules Harlow, with contributions from Tamara Cohen, Rochelle Furstenberg, Rabbi Daniel Gordis, Leora Tanenbaum, and many others
A guide to traditional Jewish prayer enriched with insight and wisdom from a broad variety of viewpoints—from Orthodox, Conservative, Reform, and Reconstructionist Judaism to New Age and feminist.
8½ x 11, 400 pp, Quality PB, ISBN 1-58023-163-2 **$29.95**

My People's Prayer Book Series
Traditional Prayers, Modern Commentaries *Edited by Rabbi Lawrence A. Hoffman*
Provides diverse and exciting commentary to the traditional liturgy, helping modern men and women find new wisdom in Jewish prayer, and bring liturgy into their lives. Each book includes Hebrew text, modern translation, and commentaries from all perspectives of the Jewish world.
Vol. 1—The *Sh'ma* and Its Blessings
7 x 10, 168 pp, Hardcover, ISBN 1-879045-79-6 **$24.99**
Vol. 2—The *Amidah*
7 x 10, 240 pp, Hardcover, ISBN 1-879045-80-X **$24.95**
Vol. 3—*P'sukei D'zimrah* (Morning Psalms)
7 x 10, 240 pp, Hardcover, ISBN 1-879045-81-8 **$24.95**
Vol. 4—*Seder K'riat Hatorah* (The Torah Service)
7 x 10, 264 pp, Hardcover, ISBN 1-879045-82-6 **$23.95**
Vol. 5—*Birkhot Hashachar* (Morning Blessings)
7 x 10, 240 pp, Hardcover, ISBN 1-879045-83-4 **$24.95**
Vol. 6—*Tachanun* and Concluding Prayers
7 x 10, 240 pp, Hardcover, ISBN 1-879045-84-2 **$24.95**
Vol. 7—Shabbat at Home
7 x 10, 240 pp, Hardcover, ISBN 1-879045-85-0 **$24.95**
Vol. 8—*Kabbalat Shabbat* (Welcoming Shabbat in the Synagogue)
7 x 10, 240 pp, Hardcover, ISBN 1-58023-121-7 **$24.99**

Spirituality/Women's Interest

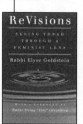

The Quotable Jewish Woman: Wisdom, Inspiration & Humor from the Mind & Heart *Edited and compiled by Elaine Bernstein Partnow*
The definitive collection of ideas, reflections, humor, and wit of over 300 Jewish women.
6 x 9, 496 pp, Hardcover, ISBN 1-58023-193-4 **$29.99**

Lifecycles, Vol. 1: Jewish Women on Life Passages & Personal Milestones
Edited and with introductions by Rabbi Debra Orenstein 6 x 9, 480 pp, Quality PB, ISBN 1-58023-018-0 **$19.95**

Lifecycles, Vol. 2: Jewish Women on Biblical Themes in Contemporary Life
Edited and with introductions by Rabbi Debra Orenstein and Rabbi Jane Rachel Litman
6 x 9, 464 pp, Quality PB, ISBN 1-58023-019-9 **$19.95**

Moonbeams: A Hadassah Rosh Hodesh Guide *Edited by Carol Diament, Ph.D.*
8½ x 11, 240 pp, Quality PB, ISBN 1-58023-099-7 **$20.00**

ReVisions: Seeing Torah through a Feminist Lens *By Rabbi Elyse Goldstein*
5½ x 8½, 224 pp, Quality PB, ISBN 1-58023-117-9 **$16.95**

White Fire: A Portrait of Women Spiritual Leaders in America
By Rabbi Malka Drucker. Photographs by Gay Block.
7 x 10, 320 pp, 30+ b/w photos, Hardcover, ISBN 1-893361-64-0 **$24.95** *(A SkyLight Paths book)*

Women of the Wall: Claiming Sacred Ground at Judaism's Holy Site
Edited by Phyllis Chesler and Rivka Haut 6 x 9, 496 pp, b/w photos, Hardcover, ISBN 1-58023-161-6 **$34.95**

The Women's Haftarah Commentary: New Insights from Women Rabbis on the 54 Weekly Haftarah Portions, the 5 Megillot & Special Shabbatot
Edited by Rabbi Elyse Goldstein 6 x 9, 560 pp, Hardcover, ISBN 1-58023-133-0 **$39.99**

The Women's Torah Commentary: New Insights from Women Rabbis on the 54 Weekly Torah Portions *Edited by Rabbi Elyse Goldstein*
6 x 9, 496 pp, Hardcover, ISBN 1-58023-076-8 **$34.95**

The Year Mom Got Religion: One Woman's Midlife Journey into Judaism
By Lee Meyerhoff Hendler 6 x 9, 208 pp, Quality PB, ISBN 1-58023-070-9 **$15.95**

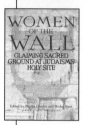

See Holidays for *The Women's Passover Companion: Women's Reflections on the Festival of Freedom* and *The Women's Seder Sourcebook: Rituals & Readings for Use at the Passover Seder.* Also see Bar/Bat Mitzvah for *The JGirl's Guide: The Young Jewish Woman's Handbook for Coming of Age.*

Travel

Israel—A Spiritual Travel Guide, 2nd Edition
A Companion for the Modern Jewish Pilgrim
By Rabbi Lawrence A. Hoffman 4¾ x 10, 256 pp, Quality PB, illus., ISBN 1-58023-261-2 **$18.99**
Also Available: **The Israel Mission Leader's Guide** ISBN 1-58023-085-7 **$4.95**

12 Steps

100 Blessings Every Day Daily Twelve Step Recovery Affirmations, Exercises for Personal Growth & Renewal Reflecting Seasons of the Jewish Year
By Rabbi Kerry M. Olitzky. Foreword by Rabbi Neil Gillman.
One-day-at-a-time monthly format. Reflects on the rhythm of the Jewish calendar to bring insight to recovery from addictions.
4½ x 6¼, 432 pp, Quality PB, ISBN 1-879045-30-3 **$15.99**

Recovery from Codependence: A Jewish Twelve Steps Guide to Healing Your Soul
By Rabbi Kerry M. Olitzky 6 x 9, 160 pp, Quality PB, ISBN 1-879045-32-X **$13.95**

Renewed Each Day: Daily Twelve Step Recovery Meditations Based on the Bible
By Rabbi Kerry M. Olitzky and Aaron Z.
Vol. 1—Genesis & Exodus: 6 x 9, 224 pp, Quality PB, ISBN 1-879045-12-5 **$14.95**
Vol. 2—Leviticus, Numbers & Deuteronomy: 6 x 9, 280 pp, Quality PB, ISBN 1-879045-13-3 **$14.95**

Twelve Jewish Steps to Recovery: A Personal Guide to Turning from Alcoholism & Other Addictions—Drugs, Food, Gambling, Sex...
By Rabbi Kerry M. Olitzky and Stuart A. Copans, M.D. Preface by Abraham J. Twerski, M.D.
6 x 9, 144 pp, Quality PB, ISBN 1-879045-09-5 **$14.95**

Theology/Philosophy

Aspects of Rabbinic Theology
By Solomon Schechter. New Introduction by Dr. Neil Gillman.
6 x 9, 448 pp, Quality PB, ISBN 1-879045-24-9 **$19.95**

Broken Tablets: Restoring the Ten Commandments and Ourselves
Edited by Rachel S. Mikva. Introduction by Lawrence Kushner. Afterword by Arnold Jacob Wolf.
6 x 9, 192 pp, Quality PB, ISBN 1-58023-158-6 **$16.95**; Hardcover, ISBN 1-58023-066-0 **$21.95**

Creating an Ethical Jewish Life
A Practical Introduction to Classic Teachings on How to Be a Jew
By Dr. Byron L. Sherwin and Seymour J. Cohen
6 x 9, 336 pp, Quality PB, ISBN 1-58023-114-4 **$19.95**

The Death of Death: Resurrection and Immortality in Jewish Thought
By Dr. Neil Gillman 6 x 9, 336 pp, Quality PB, ISBN 1-58023-081-4 **$18.95**

Evolving Halakhah: A Progressive Approach to Traditional Jewish Law
By Rabbi Dr. Moshe Zemer
6 x 9, 480 pp, Quality PB, ISBN 1-58023-127-6 **$29.95**; Hardcover, ISBN 1-58023-002-4 **$40.00**

Hasidic Tales: Annotated & Explained
By Rabbi Rami Shapiro. Foreword by Andrew Harvey, SkyLight Illuminations series editor.
5½ x 8½, 240 pp, Quality PB, ISBN 1-893361-86-1 **$16.95** (A SkyLight Paths Book)

A Heart of Many Rooms: Celebrating the Many Voices within Judaism
By Dr. David Hartman 6 x 9, 352 pp, Quality PB, ISBN 1-58023-156-X **$19.95**

The Hebrew Prophets: Selections Annotated & Explained
Translation & Annotation by Rabbi Rami Shapiro. Foreword by Zalman M. Schachter-Shalomi
5½ x 8½, 224 pp, Quality PB, ISBN 1-59473-037-7 **$16.99** (A SkyLight Paths book)

Keeping Faith with the Psalms: Deepen Your Relationship with God Using the
Book of Psalms By Daniel F. Polish 6 x 9, 272 pp, Hardcover, ISBN 1-58023-179-9 **$24.95**

The Last Trial
On the Legends and Lore of the Command to Abraham to Offer Isaac as a Sacrifice
By Shalom Spiegel. New Introduction by Judah Goldin.
6 x 9, 208 pp, Quality PB, ISBN 1-879045-29-X **$18.95**

A Living Covenant: The Innovative Spirit in Traditional Judaism
By Dr. David Hartman 6 x 9, 368 pp, Quality PB, ISBN 1-58023-011-3 **$18.95**

Love and Terror in the God Encounter
The Theological Legacy of Rabbi Joseph B. Soloveitchik
By Dr. David Hartman
6 x 9, 240 pp, Quality PB, ISBN 1-58023-176-4 **$19.95**; Hardcover, ISBN 1-58023-112-8 **$25.00**

Seeking the Path to Life
Theological Meditations on God and the Nature of People, Love, Life and Death
By Rabbi Ira F. Stone 6 x 9, 160 pp, Quality PB, ISBN 1-879045-47-8 **$14.95**

The Spirit of Renewal: Finding Faith after the Holocaust
By Rabbi Edward Feld 6 x 9, 224 pp, Quality PB, ISBN 1-879045-40-0 **$16.95**

Tormented Master: The Life and Spiritual Quest of Rabbi Nahman of Bratslav
By Dr. Arthur Green 6 x 9, 416 pp, Quality PB, ISBN 1-879045-11-7 **$19.99**

Your Word Is Fire: The Hasidic Masters on Contemplative Prayer
Edited and translated by Dr. Arthur Green and Barry W. Holtz
6 x 9, 160 pp, Quality PB, ISBN 1-879045-25-7 **$15.95**

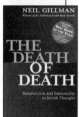
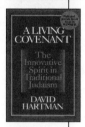

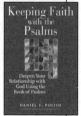

I Am Jewish
Personal Reflections Inspired by the Last Words of Daniel Pearl

Almost 150 Jews—both famous and not—from all walks of life, from all around
the world, write about Identity, Heritage, Covenant / Chosenness and Faith,
Humanity and Ethnicity, and *Tikkun Olam* and Justice.

Edited by Judea and Ruth Pearl
6 x 9, 304 pp, Deluxe PB w/flaps, ISBN 1-58023-259-0 **$18.99**; Hardcover, ISBN 1-58023-183-7 **$24.99**
Download a free copy of the *I Am Jewish Teacher's Guide* at our website:
www.jewishlights.com

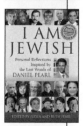

About Jewish Lights

People of all faiths and backgrounds yearn for books that attract, engage, educate, and spiritually inspire.

Our principal goal is to stimulate thought and help all people learn about who the Jewish People are, where they come from, and what the future can be made to hold. While people of our diverse Jewish heritage are the primary audience, our books speak to people in the Christian world as well and will broaden their understanding of Judaism and the roots of their own faith.

We bring to you authors who are at the forefront of spiritual thought and experience. While each has something different to say, they all say it in a voice that you can hear.

Our books are designed to welcome you and then to engage, stimulate, and inspire. We judge our success not only by whether or not our books are beautiful and commercially successful, but by whether or not they make a difference in your life.

For your information and convenience, at the back of this book we have provided a list of other Jewish Lights books you might find interesting and useful. They cover all the categories of your life:

Bar/Bat Mitzvah	Life Cycle
Bible Study / Midrash	Meditation
Children's Books	Parenting
Congregation Resources	Prayer
Current Events / History	Ritual / Sacred Practice
Ecology	Spirituality
Fiction: Mystery, Science Fiction	Theology / Philosophy
Grief / Healing	Travel
Holidays / Holy Days	Twelve Steps
Inspiration	Women's Interest
Kabbalah / Mysticism / Enneagram	

Stuart M. Matlins, Publisher

Or phone, fax, mail or e-mail to: **JEWISH LIGHTS Publishing**
Sunset Farm Offices, Route 4 • P.O. Box 237 • Woodstock, Vermont 05091
Tel: (802) 457-4000 • Fax: (802) 457-4004 • www.jewishlights.com
Credit card orders: **(800) 962-4544** (8:30AM–5:30PM ET Monday–Friday)
Generous discounts on quantity orders. SATISFACTION GUARANTEED. Prices subject to change.

For more information about each book, visit our website at www.jewishlights.com